DON'T ROCK THE BOAT

DON'T ROCK THE BOAT

by Robin Hawdon

WARNER CHAPPELL PLAYS

LONDON

A Time Warner Company

First published in 1992
by Warner Chappell Plays Ltd
129 Park Street, London W1Y 3FA

ISBN 0 85676 158 3

Cover Design by Helen Lannaghan.
Printed by Commercial Colour Press, London E7.

Don't Rock the Boat was first presented by Redgrave Theatre Productions at the Redgrave Theatre, Farnham on 1 April, 1992, with the following cast:

Arthur Bullhead   Michael Sharvell-Martin

Mary Bullhead   Pauline Yates

Shirley Bullhead   Sarah Reed

John Coombes   Garfield Morgan

Carol Coombes   Jane Rossington

Wendy Coombes   Sally Geoghegan

Directed by Graham Watkins
Designed by Janey Gardiner
Lighting Designed by Mark Doubleday

The action takes place on *The Bunty*, a converted barge, moored on a quiet stretch of the Thames, somewhere in Berkshire.

ACT ONE

ACT TWO

CAST

ARTHUR BULLHEAD	Middle-aged businessman
MARY BULLHEAD	His wife
SHIRLEY BULLHEAD	Their daughter, 17
JOHN COOMBES	Middle-aged solicitor
CAROL COOMBES	His wife
WENDY COOMBES	Their daughter, 17

SETTING

The scene is a converted barge, *'The Bunty'*, moored on a quiet stretch of the Thames somewhere in Berkshire. The boat is spacious and immaculate, having been expensively, if rather flashily converted to make a holiday home. Only the front two-thirds can be seen, in cut-away section, viewed as from mid-stream with the river bank behind it. There is a small fore-deck, stage left, with gangplank to the bank beyond the boat, ladder up onto the main roof deck, where are scattered a couple of sun mattresses or loungers, and steps down to the main saloon. This is centre stage, comfortably, if too cosily furnished, with chintzy soft furnishings, and much brass, teak and nautical embellishment about the place. It is lit by circular brass portholes looking out onto the bank. A collapsible dining table is upstage, surrounded on two sides by built-in cushioned seating. All this converts into a double bunk when required. Next to this, a small galley, with sink, cooker, fridge, etc, is built in, beside which is an upstage bulkhead door to a passageway leading to the rest of the boat. There are a couple of easy chairs downstage, and various boating magazines and books on sailing are in evidence around the place.

The small 'guest cabin' is stage right, next door to the saloon, with upstage door to the passageway. It has a double bunk, and downstage door leading to offstage 'en suite' toilet and shower room.

ACT ONE

Scene One

A warm summer's afternoon. The sounds of the river - water, bird cries, boat creaks. No one is about. The perfect peace is spoilt by the distant sound of a car arriving and parking some way off. Door slams and faint voices. As they approach the dialogue becomes discernible.

ARTHUR   (*off*) Right, Shirley, you bring those. Mary, you bring that lot. And mind those bags - they'll split if you're not careful. Christ, there's enough here to feed an army! What've you got in 'em?

MARY   (*off*) Well, you'd be the first to complain if we ran out, Arthur.

ARTHUR   I know you though. Bought all sorts of rubbish we don't need. Why you can never make a sensible list before you go shopping, beats me. Get round in half the time, buy half the stuff, and cause half the aggro.

            (SHIRLEY *appears on the river bank, loaded with carrier bags.*)

            Look out, there's cow pats around. I don't want anyone treading crap around the boat after I've just got it ship-shape.

SHIRLEY   (*muttering*) There's enough crap around already.

            (ARTHUR *appears carrying a box of drinks.* MARY *follows with more carrier bags.*)

ARTHUR   What d'you say? If you've got anything to say, girl, let's all hear it. Don't mutter at the ground. And do get a move on. We're late, after all that faffing around the village. They'll be here soon, and we aren't ready for them.

MARY   'Course we're ready for them. What more is there to do?

ARTHUR   What more is there . . . !

                (*He dumps his box beside the gangplank, and
                turns to harangue them.*)

                Mary, what d'you think we've got all this bloody
                stuff for, eh? What's it all for if not to try and
                contrive some semblance of civilised hospitality
                for our guests? And how d'you think that's
                going to happen, eh? Do you imagine, in your
                incorrigibly optimistic way, that if we pipe it
                aboard it will somehow all miraculously
                transform itself into a wonderful display of haute
                cuisine on its own? Eh?

MARY   Well of course not, but . . .

ARTHUR   If you'd done what I said in the first place -
                brought it all down with us, then we wouldn't
                have had this hassle - but no, you know best.
                Simpler to get it there, you said - get to know the
                local shops, you said - it's all part of the fun,
                you said - and the consequence is we spend half
                our bloody relaxing weekend clambering round
                Dickensian cobweb-ridden shelves, queuing up at
                counters run by village half-wits, and trying to
                concoct edible meals out of a lot of rubbish that
                has cost twice as much as what we can get in our
                nearest supermarket. Why is it, Mary - after
                nearly twenty years of marriage - you still cannot
                grasp the simple fact that a little bit of
                forethought and organization makes life simpler
                for yourself?

SHIRLEY   (*muttering*) And murder for everyone else.

ARTHUR   And don't you start, my girl. God help any
                husband who has to live with you! He won't
                know whether his dinner's come out of the oven,
                the dustbin, or the washing machine.

SHIRLEY   Have you finished? Because if so, can we go on
                board? We could have done it all in the amount

of time we've stood here listening to you
rabbiting on.

ARTHUR   (*bridling*) Now look . . .

MARY   (*quickly*) Oh come on, Arthur, for heaven's sake.
                (*Pushes past him onto the gangplank.*) They'll be
                here before we've unpacked the stuff at this rate.

                (SHIRLEY *starts to follow, as* MARY *totters
                nervously across with her load.*)

                Oh God, I hate this thing. It doesn't feel at all
                safe.

ARTHUR   It's perfectly safe if you just trust it and watch
                your feet. (*Grabs* SHIRLEY *by the arm.*) And . . .

SHIRLEY   Look out! You'll have the lot in the drink!

ARTHUR   . . . as I've told you a hundred times, if you go
                across one at a time.

SHIRLEY   (*exasperated*) Sorry! I forgot - all right?

ARTHUR   If you did fall in, you'd probably forget to swim.

MARY   (*feeling her way awkwardly off the end of the
                gangplank*) Watch your feet, he says. How
                you're supposed to watch your feet when your
                carrying half a ton of stuff, I don't know. Be
                very careful, Shirley.

ARTHUR   (*taking some of* SHIRLEY'S *load from her*) The
                answer is quite simple. You don't take too much
                across at one time, and you make sure you're
                evenly balanced - right?

                (SHIRLEY *follows her mother across with a bag in
                each hand. She does it with the ease of youth.*)

MARY   (*trying the cabin door, which is locked*) Hurry
                up, Arthur. The door's locked.

ARTHUR   Well of course it's locked. You don't expect me
            to leave it open to every stray passerby, do you?

            (*Picks up the box of drinks under one arm, and
            the rest of* SHIRLEY'S *load in the other, and
            staggers across the gangplank. Reaches the end,
            and almost falls as he stumbles onto the deck.*
            SHIRLEY, *who has put down her bags, catches
            him.*)

SHIRLEY   It's quite simple - don't take too much, and make
            sure you're evenly balanced.

ARTHUR   I was - we need a step putting in there. Here -
            get the keys from my left hand pocket, will you?

SHIRLEY   (*mock-flirtatious, going for his trouser pocket*)
            Oh, Dad - how intimate. Are you sure?

ARTHUR   (*angrily reacting*) Not my trousers, you idiot -
            my jacket!

            (SHIRLEY *finds the keys, and unlocks the door.*
            ARTHUR *urges them on.*)

            Right, go on then, go on.

            (*They descend the steps into the saloon.* MARY
            goes to the galley area, SHIRLEY *dumps her bags
            on the nearest chair.*)

            Not on there, girl! Cost eighteen pounds a yard,
            that material - I don't want food stains all over
            it.

            (SHIRLEY *resignedly moves the bags to the dining
            table, and then flops down with a sigh on one of
            the bench seats.*)

            And what are you sitting down for? Eh? Think
            you've finished, do you? (*She raises her eyes to
            heaven.*) Get that lot unloaded, girl, and then lay
            the table for tea. Mother, you get on with the
            dinner - I'll sort out the drinks. As I've said, I

don't want to have us all clattering dishes,
peeling potatoes and God knows what, the
moment they arrive.

SHIRLEY   What are we going to do then - sit round and sing
"For Those In Peril On The Sea"?

(MARY *titters with her.*)

ARTHUR   Is that supposed to be funny? I mean, is that the
best you can do - make facetious comments?
This weekend's as much for your benefit as ours,
you know.

SHIRLEY   Why mine?

ARTHUR   Well, she's your school friend, isn't she? (*Starts
to unpack the drinks.*)

SHIRLEY   She's not a friend. I've told you a dozen times.
I hardly know her.

ARTHUR   She's in your class, isn't she?

SHIRLEY   There are twenty nine people in my class.
They're not all bosom pals.

ARTHUR   Well, which of them *are* your friends? I've
never met any of them.

SHIRLEY   (*muttering*) Well I don't bring them home, do I?
That'd put them off me for life.

ARTHUR   And what's that supposed to mean? Are you
ashamed of your home? Eh? I bet not many of
them have got a home like that to go to.

SHIRLEY   No - that's the point.

ARTHUR   What? What's that?

MARY   (*intervening*) Oh come on, you two. Arthur,
what kind of potatoes do you want with the steak
au poivre tonight?

ARTHUR   I don't know. I leave that sort of thing to you.

MARY   I think I'll do saute then.

ARTHUR   We've bought new, haven't we? You don't want
            to waste new potatoes by sauteeing them.

MARY   (*long suffering*) All right, I'll do new.

ARTHUR   With some mint. Don't forget the mint.

MARY   I'm glad you left it to me, Arthur.

ARTHUR   (*to* SHIRLEY) What I don't understand is, what
            have you got against this girl? I mean we met
            her through you. We got to know her parents
            through you.

SHIRLEY   I only introduced you on Sports Day because you
            wanted to meet them. She's no particular friend
            of mine.

ARTHUR   Why, what's wrong with her?

SHIRLEY   There's nothing wrong with her! She's just not
            my type, that's all. She's a wimp.

ARTHUR   And what's a wimp when it's at home?

SHIRLEY   Well, she's just wet. She's no go about her.

ARTHUR   You mean she's well-mannered, and speaks
            normally, and doesn't dress like a freak.
            (SHIRLEY *sighs*.) Unlike that dropout gang you
            mix with, who hang round the pubs and the
            discos, when they should be working for their
            'A' levels - eh? I've seen them. All into freaky
            clothes and soft drugs and hard sex.

SHIRLEY   Oh for God's sake! Are we going to start that
            one again?

MARY   Arthur, please. Are you going to have another
            family row, just when these people are about to
            arrive?

ARTHUR   Look, all I'm saying is . . . Mary, that
            cupboard's for pans, not vegetables. It's not like
            being at home, you know, where you've got
            enough space to accommodate your eccentric
            ideas of storage . . . All I'm saying is, they're a
            very nice family, and I want us all to enjoy the
            weekend, including Shirley. I don't know why
            she's so against having them, that's all.

SHIRLEY   I'm not against having them. I'm just against
            having to share this bed . . . (*Indicating the
            benches she's sitting on.*) . . . with Wendy
            Coombes just because you want to get in thick
            with her father.

ARTHUR   Ah - now we're getting to it. What do you mean
            by that?

SHIRLEY   Well, you made no bones about it. You wanted
            to meet him. Just because he's a councillor and
            on the Planning Board or Committee, or
            whatever it is. This whole weekend's simply so
            you can pull a few strings and do some clever
            property deal or other.

ARTHUR   That's not true. That's not true at all. He can be
            useful to me, yes, but that's not the only reason
            we've asked them. They're intelligent, cultured
            people. They're the sort of people your mother
            and I like to mix with - aren't they, Mary?

MARY   Don't ask me - I hardly know them.

ARTHUR   (*getting angrier*) Yes, they are! You said you
            liked them very much.

MARY   Well, yes - the couple of times we've met them . . .

ARTHUR   Well, then. And if I can combine business and
            pleasure, then that's all to the good, isn't it? I
            mean I can't just knock off work and laze around
            the river like "Wind In The Willows" whenever I
            feel like it, you know. What d'you think's
            bought all this in the first place? Hard work, and

having the right ideas, and getting to know the right people, that's what. (*Searches in a cupboard.*) Mary, where the hell are all our glasses?

MARY   (*busy in the galley area*) Don't ask me, dear.

ARTHUR   Well I *am* asking you. I stocked this place up with plenty of glasses when we took it over, and now there's half of them missing. (*Searches in the galley cupboards.*) They're either smashed or in the wrong place, and there's no prizes for who's to blame for that. (*Straightens up, holding a pack of toilet rolls.*) What the hell . . . ? This is the crockery cupboard! What in God's name is it stuffed full of toilet rolls for? Is it because we're going to eat our tea off toilet tissue, or because we're all going to crap in the sink from now on?

MARY   (*taking them*) Oh, Arthur, please . . . I just put them in there for the moment to get them out of the way.

ARTHUR   Typical example, you see? Dump everything in the nearest convenient place, and then you wonder why no one can find anything to eat off, or anything to wipe their bottoms with! The place for those is in the cupboard in our bathroom. How many times do I have to tell you?

(MARY *takes them off along the passageway to the cabins.* ARTHUR *rummages once more in the cupboards.*)

It's the same at home. If ever you want anything, the secret is to look in the most unlikely place you can think of, and ten-to-one there it'll be.

(*Triumphantly unearths a couple of glasses.*)

Ah! What did I tell you? In amongst the bloody cleaning stuff! And then everyone wonders why their gin and tonic tastes of Harpic and brass polish.

(*Flings a tea towel over his shoulder, and rinses the glasses under the tap.*)

Come on, Shirley, get a move on. I want the tea laid out, so all we have to do is put the kettle on when they get here.

SHIRLEY   Well I can't do anything while you're messing about there, I need to get to the cupboards.

ARTHUR   (*moving aside with the glasses*) There you are then. If you can't find any crockery, you'll probably have to look in the food cupboard, and vice-versa. How your mother manages to run a household at all beats me. (*Looks around.*) Where's the tea towel? Who's moved that now? Where's the bloody tea towel?

SHIRLEY   On your shoulder.

ARTHUR   Oh. (*Takes it, and polishes the glasses.*) What's the time? (*Looks at the cabin clock.*) Twenty past four. Where are they? They should be here by now.

SHIRLEY   We only said around four o'clock, Dad. We weren't specific.

ARTHUR   No, that's your trouble, you never are specific. You're so unspecific it's a wonder you can tell the difference between night and day.

SHIRLEY   Well it's meant to be a casual weekend, isn't it? Not a bloody military exercise.

ARTHUR   And don't use that language at me, young woman. I've told you about that before. I bet Wendy Coombes doesn't swear in front of her parents.

SHIRLEY   Oh God, we're going to have that all weekend,
              are we?

ARTHUR   What?

SHIRLEY   (*mimicking*) Look how nicely behaved Wendy is,
              Shirley. *She* doesn't belch across the tea table
              when we've got guests.

ARTHUR   Is that supposed to be a funny remark? Is that
              really the level of your humour - eh?

SHIRLEY   (*sighing*) No, Dad.

ARTHUR   I don't understand you. I really don't.

MARY   (*calling, off*) Arthur! Come here, will you?

ARTHUR   (*shouting back*) Now what?

MARY   (*off*) The loo seems to be blocked, or something.

ARTHUR   Oh, my God! Who's buggered *that* up then?

SHIRLEY   Language, father.

              (*He glares at her, and stomps off. She moodily
              sets about throwing tea things casually onto the
              table. The* COOMBES *family appears on the river
              bank, carrying various suitcases.*)

CAROL   This is it. 'The Bunty'. (*Puts down her case,
              and breathes a sigh of relief.*) Oh, thank
              heavens! They didn't tell us it was so far from
              the road.

JOHN   Good thing, really. More quiet. Lovely spot,
              isn't it?

WENDY   Oh, isn't it a pretty boat?

JOHN   Looks like a converted barge, or something.
              (*Peers at the portholes.*) I can't see anyone
              about.

CAROL   Where do you suppose we'll sleep, darling? I
           hope we'll have our own bedroom.

JOHN   Well of course we will.

CAROL   I thought we might be in hammocks down in the
           bottom, or something.

JOHN   We're not sailing with Nelson, darling - it'll all
           be highly civilised. If I know anything about
           Arthur Bullhead, probably quite flash as well.

WENDY   Oh God, I'm dreading this!

CAROL   Why, darling? It'll be fun.

WENDY   It's just that Shirley Bullhead's so different to
           me. I gather we've got to share a cabin, or
           something.

CAROL   I'm sure she's a very nice girl. Her manner's
           probably just insecurity.

JOHN   Not surprising with a father like that.

CAROL   Why, what's wrong with him?

JOHN   Oh, he's rather the domineering type, that's all.
           Witness how he bulldozed us into this trip.

CAROL   I thought it was very hospitable of him.

JOHN   And to be honest, I'm not quite sure of his
           motives. Still, you're right - we mustn't be
           unfair. (*Picks up his case.*) Come on - let's see
           if there's anyone on board.

           (*They move to the gangplank.*)

CAROL   (*nervously*) Oh heavens - have we got to walk
           across that?

JOHN   (*testing it*) It's pretty solid. Come on.

(*He crosses the gangplank, and then turns to help the others, taking their suitcases, and then holding out a hand for them to grab as they awkwardly totter across. Whilst this is going on* ARTHUR *and* MARY *return along the passage, in the middle of a furious row. Their voices can be heard for some time before they appear. The* COOMBES *become aware of the noise, and stop to listen.*)

ARTHUR   It's like talking to a bloody brick wall! I mean, why do I bother? You tell me, why do I bother?

MARY   Arthur, don't take it out on her, please. We don't know it was her.

ARTHUR   Of course it was her! I mean who else smokes cigarettes round here - the bloody swans? (*Storms into the saloon.*) How many times, young woman - how many times have you been told not to put anything down these toilets?

SHIRLEY   Me?

ARTHUR   Well of course you! Who else d'you think I'm talking to? Time and time again I've said, don't put anything down the toilets because they're not the same as the ones at home, and they'll block up. And what happens? Last time it was a bloody sanitary towel, and this time it's a cigarette packet! And don't tell me they weren't yours, because neither your mother nor me uses cigarettes or sanitary towels.

SHIRLEY   Well, what else was I supposed to do with them?

ARTHUR   I don't know! Dispose of them - that's what people normally do, isn't it?

SHIRLEY   There isn't anywhere to dispose of them! Didn't think of putting waste bins in the toilets, did you, when you were dreaming up this stupid boat?

ARTHUR   You shouldn't be smoking in the bloody toilets!
            You shouldn't be smoking anywhere, as I've said
            a million times.

MARY   Leave her alone, for heaven's sake, Arthur. It's
            our fault for not thinking of the bins anyway.

ARTHUR   Oh, it's our fault now, is it? Wonderful! I might
            have known it would end up being our fault.
            What's she doing smoking at her age anyway?
            Or using sanitary towels for that matter?

SHIRLEY   Christ!

MARY   Well she can't help being a woman, can she?
            What can she do about her periods if there aren't
            any bins around?

ARTHUR   *I* don't know. Why can't she time the bloody
            things better, or something?

            (SHIRLEY'S *temper bursts, and she hurls a plate
            across the saloon, smashing it against the wall.
            Deathly silence as they all stare at the pieces.*
            JOHN COOMBES *knocks hesitantly on the saloon
            door. The* BULLHEADS *turn to stare at that.*)

ARTHUR   Oh, my God! (*Hesitates, then gestures at the
            broken pieces of crockery.*) Quick - get that out
            of the way!

            (MARY *moves to pick them up.* ARTHUR *goes to the
            door, and opens it.*)

JOHN   Er . . . hello. We've arrived.

ARTHUR   Well, hello there! Good timing. Bang on to
            catch our daily family jousting match - ha, ha!
            You're lucky. We normally charge admission,
            you know.

JOHN   (*entering the saloon*) We thought we heard
            something, but we weren't quite sure.

CAROL   (*following*) We thought you must be playing a
           game. We couldn't hear what you were saying,
           of course.

ARTHUR   You mustn't mind us. It's all part of our
           domestic fun and frolics. Come in, come in.
           You remember Mary, don't you?

MARY   (*turning from the waste bin, where she has been
           dumping the broken crockery*) Welcome aboard.

JOHN   Nice to see you again.

CAROL   It's so kind of you to invite us.

ARTHUR   Not at all. We love having people here, don't
           we, Mary? It's what the boat is for. Say hello to
           Wendy, Shirl.

SHIRLEY   (*dour*) Hello.

WENDY   Hello, Shirley.

CAROL   Isn't it beautiful? What a beautiful boat! (*Takes
           her husband's arm.*) Isn't it, John?

JOHN   Superb.

ARTHUR   Well, we've worked quite hard at it. You should
           have seen it when I bought it. (*Surreptitiously
           kicks a bit of broken plate under a chair.*)

JOHN   Oh, you've done the conversion yourself then?

ARTHUR   A hulk! It was nothing but a hulk. Wasn't it,
           Mary?

MARY   Well, more or less.

CAROL   Well, it's beautiful now. Oh, look at the
           kitchen! Isn't that neat?

ARTHUR   Galley. You call it a galley on board a boat.
           You'll have to get these seafaring terms right,

you know, Carol - ha, ha. (*Hides some bits of shopping which got overlooked.*) Yes, I found it at the moorings down at Shepperton. Hell of a state it was in - picked it up for a song. Always been a dream of ours to have a boat, hasn't it, Mary?

MARY   Well, a dream of yours.

ARTHUR   And a good solid, traditional boat too - none of your modern plastic gin palaces. (*Thumps a cross timber.*) Solid oak that is, a hundred years old!

JOHN   Splendid.

ARTHUR   And fitted out with nothing but the best. Seasoned teak, solid brass fittings. See those portholes? See those lamps? (*Gestures at* MARY *to improve on* SHIRLEY'S *laying of the tea things.*)

JOHN   Very fine.

CAROL   Did you choose all the furnishings, Mary?

MARY   Some of the furnishings. But it's really Arthur's toy.

ARTHUR   Toy? What do you mean, toy?

MARY   You know what I . . .

ARTHUR   (*laughing it off*) Some toy - sixty feet long, and weighing almost as many tons, eh? Ha, ha.

CAROL   (*peering into corners*) I love all these little cupboards and crannies. So ingenious!

ARTHUR   Well you have to make use of every bit of space on board ship, you know. (*Looks at their suitcases.*) And by Jove, you lot are going to need it, aren't you? Moving in for good, are you?

JOHN   Sorry, we have come rather over equipped. To
            be quite honest, we weren't sure what to expect,
            you see.

ARTHUR   Well, don't worry. (*Picks up their suitcases.*)
            You put the kettle on for tea, Mary, while I show
            them their cabin. Cabin, you notice, Carol. We
            don't have bedrooms here.

CAROL   Oh, right - I'll remember.

ARTHUR   Just as this is the saloon, not the lounge, parlour
            or drawing room. Wendy, you're sharing the
            dining table with Shirley.

WENDY   What?

ARTHUR   (*chuckling*) Just joking. It all folds up and pulls
            out to a very neat double bunk. Bunk, notice,
            Carol - not bed. (*She laughs.*) And the most
            comfortable one on the boat too.

WENDY   (*uncertain*) Oh, that's nice.

ARTHUR   This way. Let me show you to your quarters.

            (*He leads the way down the passage. MARY is
            busy in the galley. WENDY smiles awkwardly at
            SHIRLEY.*)

WENDY   You are lucky having a boat like this.

SHIRLEY   Do you think so?

WENDY   Well . . . yes, of course. I mean, it's lovely,
            isn't it?

SHIRLEY   Wait till you've been on it for a while before you
            make up your mind.

MARY   (*warningly*) Shirley.

            (*The door to the guest cabin opens next door,
            and ARTHUR struggles in with the cases, followed*

by CAROL *and* JOHN. *There is not much room in the confined space for all three of them.*)

ARTHUR   Bit of a tight squeeze. But that all adds to the fun, doesn't it? Ha, ha.

CAROL   Oh, it's sweet!

ARTHUR   The bunk's very comfortable - I have a thing about sleeping arrangements. But don't rock the boat too much, or you could have us over - ha, ha. (*They don't respond.*) Er - you can stow some of your clothes in there. Oh, and don't open the porthole if there's anything over a force eight gale blowing.

CAROL   Surely you don't . . .

ARTHUR   Just joking. (*Goes to the shower room door.*)

MARY   (*next door*) Sit down, Wendy. Make yourself comfortable.

WENDY   (*sitting at the table*) Thank you.

ARTHUR   (*opening the shower room door*) And here's your own private toilet and shower room.

CAROL   Oh, isn't that clever? Look, John - it's so neat!

JOHN   Splendid.

ARTHUR   (*disappearing inside*) Now - very important - there's one thing you must learn, and that's how to work the head.

CAROL   (*following*) The what?

(*There is no room for* JOHN, *so he stays watching from the cabin. There are muffled instructions from* ARTHUR.)

MARY   (*over this*) Open that cake, will you, Shirley - and put it on the plate. (*Hands a bought cake to*

SHIRLEY.) Sorry, it's only a shop one, Wendy. I didn't have time to do any cooking before we came down.

SHIRLEY   She can't make cakes to save her life anyway.

MARY   Shirley!

WENDY   (*quickly*) It looks lovely.

            (*There is the sound of a toilet flushing, and
            ARTHUR and CAROL re-emerge from the shower
            room.*)

ARTHUR   . . . and most important of all - you mustn't put anything down it.

CAROL   (*uncertainly*) Anything down it?

ARTHUR   No. Well, what I mean is, anything bigger than, er . . . you'd send down in the natural way of things, if you get my meaning.

CAROL   Oh, yes, I see.

ARTHUR   Temperamental little bastards, they are. Always having to unbung them if you're not careful.

CAROL   (*with distaste*) Oh dear.

ARTHUR   Well now, have a quick wash and brush-up if you need it, and then come along and have some tea.

CAROL   Oh, thank you. I'm dying for a cup of tea.

ARTHUR   Laced with rum and accompanied by ship's biscuits and weevils - ha, ha.

            (ARTHUR *goes out. They look at each other.*)

CAROL   Well, it's very nice, isn't it, John?

JOHN   Yes. To be honest, it's not quite my taste, but they've obviously spent a fair bit on it.

CAROL   Is he very well off then, do you think?

JOHN   (*going into the shower room - sound of running water*) Oh, he does all right, Arthur Bullhead. Fingers in many pies.

CAROL   Nothing illegal, surely?

JOHN   Oh no, in all honesty I wouldn't say that. Just a very clever wheeler-dealer. (*Re-emerges.*) Mostly property, and there's a lot of money in that if you get it right.

CAROL   Well, it's very nice of them to ask us, anyway. (*Hugs him adoringly.*) Oh darling, won't this be fun?

JOHN   (*not so sure*) Yes.

CAROL   Excuse me, I must just pay a visit. (*Goes into the shower room.*) Oh dear, I hope I can use this thing.

           (*Closes the door. He opens his suitcase to unpack.* ARTHUR *appears in the saloon.*)

ARTHUR   Right now - tea ready?

MARY   Won't be long.

ARTHUR   (*muttering*) Don't forget to put in some of that Earl Grey.

MARY   Don't fuss, Arthur.

ARTHUR   Well now, Wendy - what do you think of life afloat?

SHIRLEY   Give her a chance. She's only just got here.

WENDY   It's lovely. Must be wonderful to have all this to come to.

ARTHUR   Well, it's nice. As you get older, Wendy, you'll
              learn the importance of having outside interests.
              (SHIRLEY *raises her eyes to the ceiling.*) Shirley
              doesn't appreciate it yet, but she's very lucky to
              have somewhere like this to come to - change the
              scene, escape from the monotony of home life.

SHIRLEY   That's true.

MARY   (*bringing the teapot*) Here we are.

ARTHUR   Where are those tea cakes?

MARY   They're coming - give me a chance. Are John
              and Carol coming?

ARTHUR   They won't be a minute. Shall I cut the cake?
              (*Reaches for a knife.*) Where's that good knife,
              Mary? This thing's no good.

MARY   I don't know. What's wrong with that?

ARTHUR   (*holding it up*) Well look at it. That's for
              spreading butter, not cutting things. (MARY
              rummages in the drawers for the other knife.)
              I'm always trying to teach these two, Wendy -
              use the right tool for the right job, and you save
              yourself no end of trouble. That's a simple rule
              of life that your father will understand.

WENDY   Oh, he's not very good with his hands.

ARTHUR   That's not the point.   I bet his office is a model
              of efficiency. He couldn't be a successful
              solicitor, and have time for all his other
              activities, unless it was. I bet his fax machine is
              as up to date as his filing system. I bet his
              secretary has the latest word processor, and
              his . . .

WENDY   I think she uses a very old typewriter actually.
              (*He stares at her, non-plussed.*) But it is a very
              good one.

ARTHUR   I bet it is.

MARY   I can't find that knife, Arthur. You'll have to
              make do.

ARTHUR   See what I mean? (*Sets about cutting the cake.*)
              It'll dissolve into a pile of sawdust now.

              (CAROL *comes out of the shower room next door,
              and she and* JOHN *leave the cabin.* MARY *prepares
              to pour tea.*)

              And do use the tea strainer when we're having
              Earl Grey, Mary. I can't stand having bits
              floating round the top - it's like drinking ants.
              (JOHN *and* CAROL *appear.*) Ah, there you are!
              Tea's ready. Come and sit down. Everything all
              right?

CAROL   Yes, fine thank you.

ARTHUR   You squeeze in there, Carol. John, you go at the
              end.

JOHN   Right.

ARTHUR   Pour them some tea, Mary.

MARY   (*already doing so*) What do you think I'm
              doing?

ARTHUR   Help yourself to everything - it's every man for
              himself here. We don't stand on ceremony in
              our family.

SHIRLEY   We just stand on each other.

              (WENDY *splutters with amusement.*)

ARTHUR   (*grim*) Now then, Shirley. None of your high
              school humour here.

SHIRLEY   Comprehensive, Dad. We don't have high
              schools any more. Ask Mr Coombes.

ARTHUR   You know what I mean. Now then, everybody -
            here's the programme for today. Leisurely tea
            now - get us in training for the rest of the
            weekend, ha, ha. Then a bit nearer opening
            time, I thought those who want to might like to
            stretch their legs along the river bank towards
            the Bargeman's Arms. Nice little pub half a
            mile or so down river. John, Carol - what do you
            say?

CAROL   Oh, that sounds nice - doesn't it, John?

JOHN   Good idea.

ARTHUR   Girls - do you want to come?

SHIRLEY   Only if we can have a proper drink. I'm not
            going to drink coca-cola all evening.

ARTHUR   What rules do you have about that, John?

JOHN   Well, we make an exception for special
            occasions. And in holiday time.

ARTHUR   Well all right then - glass of wine just this once.
            As long as it doesn't get your father struck off,
            Wendy - ha, ha. Mary, are you coming?

MARY   I think I'll stay and get the dinner ready, Arthur.

CAROL   Oh, you must come, Mary.

JOHN   Yes, indeed.

MARY   I'd really rather. I can have it all ready for when
            you get back.

ARTHUR   That's probably the best plan. She's not a pub-
            goer, Mary. Right then - it's a noggin or two at
            the Bargeman's, and then back here for dinner
            about eight. Avocado with prawns and
            Bullhead's special sauce; steak au poivre, new
            potatoes, and petits pois a là Bird's Eye;
            followed by some revolting frozen strawberry

cream gateau that looks like it fell off
somebody's head at Ascot. It's convenience
food par excellence this weekend, I'm afraid -
we didn't have time to do any proper shopping.
However we do have a rather nice little Côtes du
Rhone to wash it down with, and even a drop of
Remy Martin to help us kid ourselves it was all
haute cuisine.

CAROL   It all sounds lovely.

SHIRLEY   And then afterwards Wendy and me can go for a
walk round the village.

(*Pause. Everyone looks at her.*)

ARTHUR   What?

SHIRLEY   Just do a bit of exploring. It's going to be a nice
evening.

ARTHUR   What do you want to see the village for? You've
always said it was a dead end place.

SHIRLEY   It is, but you lot will be talking business and
stuff all night. That's no fun for us.

ARTHUR   You've never been one for evening strolls round
country villages. What are you up to, young
woman?

MARY   Oh, Arthur, don't be so suspicious. What's
wrong with it?

ARTHUR   I don't know. There's something fishy going on.

SHIRLEY   Oh, Christ . . .

ARTHUR   Wandering around on their own on a Saturday
night - I don't like that idea. John - what do you
say?

JOHN   Well . . . I don't know. How far is it?

ARTHUR	Quite a way. Along the towpath, and up the road.
SHIRLEY	It's less than half a mile. Don't be so old fashioned, Dad.
ARTHUR	I'm just being sensible. Wendy, do you want to go?
WENDY	Well, I . . . (*Looks at* SHIRLEY, *who winks at her conspiratorially.*) It might be quite fun.
MARY	Oh, come on, Arthur. You said you wanted them to get on together.
ARTHUR	I know Shirley. They're up to something.
SHIRLEY	What? Soliciting in the village High Street? Taking clients in the churchyard?
ARTHUR	(*angry*) And there's no need for that kind of talk, young woman! That's not funny. What on earth do you suppose our guests are thinking of you?
CAROL	It's all right. We know she was only joking.
ARTHUR	Well it's not a joke I appreciate. Do you hear me, Shirley?
SHIRLEY	(*long suffering*) Yes, Dad.
ARTHUR	We'll discuss this evening later. I'm not at all sure about it.
SHIRLEY	(*rising from the table*) I'm going up on deck. It's so stuffy in here. Coming, Wendy?
WENDY	(*awkwardly, looking at her parents*) Er . . .
CAROL	You go on, darling. It's a lovely day out.
WENDY	(*to* ARTHUR *and* MARY) Excuse me.
MARY	Of course, Wendy.

(WENDY *and* SHIRLEY *go out onto the deck, and
climb up the ladder onto the roof, where* SHIRLEY
sprawls out on her back in the sun.)

ARTHUR   Kids! I don't know. That's a really nice
           mannered girl you've got there, John . . . Carol.
           I don't know how you've done it. Both of ours
           are monsters.

MARY   Oh, Arthur - not all the time.

ARTHUR   Yes, they are - right little buggers! Our eldest,
           Mark - he's left home now. And not a moment
           too soon, I can tell you. It was either him or me
           by the end. Didn't want to know about his 'A'
           levels. Went straight to work for a flash London
           estate agent at the age of seventeen. And would
           you believe it - he's now on fifteen thousand a
           year, plus commission, goes by the glorified title
           of senior negotiator, and drives a new Volvo.
           And we're supposed to be in a recession! Can
           you imagine you or I commanding that at his
           age, John?

JOHN   Well, no, I . . .

ARTHUR   When I was his age I had to do a proper
           apprenticeship.

MARY   Apprenticeship?

ARTHUR   (*angrily*) Yes, apprenticeship! I had to work for
           years, learning the ropes. I didn't just slip into a
           cushy job with a nice smile on my face and a
           smart line of patter! And neither did John here -
           did you, John?

JOHN   Well, it's true that . . .

ARTHUR   I tell you, kids today have got it all too easy.
           They've never heard about learning basic
           discipline and skills, have they?

JOHN   Well, I don't think it's quite that simple.

ARTHUR   *(to* MARY*)* You see?

JOHN   I think, to be honest, it's just as tough a world
              now, but in a different way.

ARTHUR   And he should know.

JOHN   Today's youngsters have more opportunities, but
              also more competition and more demands.

ARTHUR   It's what I've been telling you for years, Mary,
              but you just won't listen.

CAROL   *(holding out her cup)* Er . . . could I have some
              more tea, do you think, please?

MARY   *(pouring)* Of course.

SHIRLEY   *(up on the top deck, staring at the sky)* I'll
              probably push my bloody father overboard before
              this weekend's finished.

WENDY   He's quite a character, isn't he?

SHIRLEY   Not the phrase I'd use.

WENDY   So what are we going to do after dinner?

SHIRLEY   *(sitting up)* There's a disco on at the village
              hall. I saw a poster for it while we were at the
              shops. It'll probably be pretty grotty, but you
              never know. There might be some local talent
              there.

WENDY   Talent?

SHIRLEY   Yes. Boys.

WENDY   *(at a loss)* Oh.

SHIRLEY   You know what boys are, don't you?

WENDY   Of course.

SHIRLEY   At any rate it's got to be more fun than hanging
            round here with our lot. I could do with a bit of
            action, couldn't you?

WENDY   Action?

SHIRLEY   Yeah. You know . . . Bit of the other. I haven't
            had a good screw all holidays.

WENDY   Oh.

SHIRLEY   Have you?

WENDY   No.

SHIRLEY   Well, then. We might as well see what the local
            stud farm's got to show us, eh?

            (*Lies back again.* WENDY *stares out over the
            river, her eyes wide. The lights fade.*)

Scene Two

*Late that evening. It is a moonlit night on the river bank.
The saloon is a warm pool of light. Everyone is sitting round
the table, where dinner has just finished.* MARY *is clearing
dishes, and bringing coffee to the table. The wine has been
flowing, and the mood is relaxed and convivial.* ARTHUR *is
holding forth.*

ARTHUR   . . . ha, ha - not a word of exaggeration, I
            promise you! Anyway . . .

JOHN   Excellent dinner, Mary.

CAROL   Hear, hear.

ARTHUR   Well, it's not the Savoy but she does all right.
            Anyway, I said to him, look, my friend, in hard
            times like these you have to use cunning or go to
            the wall. Now why don't I take over your
            development, you take over mine - we'll wind up
            both the original companies, go to different
            banks and start two new firms from scratch.
            That'll fool the lot of them!

CAROL   (*laughing*) I don't know how you stand the strain. Hanging on a knife edge all the time. John couldn't take that sort of pressure - could you, darling?

JOHN   To be honest, no. Too hair-raising by half.

CAROL   I think we like the quiet, steady life.

ARTHUR   Yes, well, I respect that, I really do. There are times, aren't there, Mary?

MARY   (*with feeling*) There certainly are.

ARTHUR   (*rising from the table*) Let's make ourselves comfortable. Bring the coffee over here, Mary.

     (*Moves down to the armchairs. The party breaks up round the table.* MARY *places the coffee tray on a side table, and then starts washing up.*)

     Now who'd like a brandy? Or perhaps a liqueur? We've got one or two here.

MARY   Oh, Arthur . . .

CAROL   Goodness! I think we've had enough.

ARTHUR   Nonsense! Nobody's driving anywhere. A little something with your coffee is obligatory. Ship's regulations.

CAROL   Oh, well . . .

SHIRLEY   No coffee for Wendy and me, Mum. We'll just pop off for a bit.

ARTHUR   Now, hold on. We haven't said you can go yet.

SHIRLEY   Oh, come on, Dad. We're only going for a walk.

ARTHUR   Where to, that's the point?

SHIRLEY   What's it matter? We don't want to sit around here watching you lot getting drunk.

MARY   They'll be all right, Arthur.

ARTHUR   Half an hour then. Then I want you back here.

SHIRLEY   Oh, don't be ridiculous!

ARTHUR   Don't you call me ridiculous, young woman!
            Half an hour's plenty for a walk. Where are you
            planning to go - Land's End?

SHIRLEY   I told you, we don't know. We might want to sit
            and talk somewhere. We don't want to have to
            rush back the moment we've . . .

ARTHUR   You can sit and talk here. You've got a whole
            boat to choose from.

SHIRLEY   We want to get off the boat. We've had enough
            of the bloody boat!

ARTHUR   You use swear words like that and you'll get
            more walking than you bargain for, my girl.
            You'll be walking the ruddy plank!

MARY   They'll be all right, Arthur. I think we can trust
            them to be responsible.

ARTHUR   Do you indeed? Well I'm not so sure.

SHIRLEY   Thanks a lot!

ARTHUR   You didn't see the types we caught them with at
            the pub.

SHIRLEY   (*sighing*) Here we go.

ARTHUR   Turned our backs for two minutes, and there they
            were being chatted up by the ugliest couple of
            punks you've ever seen.

SHIRLEY   They weren't ugly and they weren't punks. They
            were perfectly nice boys.

ARTHUR   Nice?

SHIRLEY   Just because they weren't dressed like
            Christopher Robin . . .

ARTHUR   They weren't dressed like anything I've ever
            seen! You should have seen them, Mary. You
            didn't know whether to call the police, the
            Salvation Army, or the R.S.P.C.A. (*To* SHIRLEY.)
            How did you pick them up anyway?

SHIRLEY   We didn't pick them up. I told you - one of them
            asked us the time, and we got chatting.

ARTHUR   Oh, brilliant! Highly original, that is! Eh -
            John? The moment we turn our backs they're
            being asked the time by some yobbo living on
            social security, who couldn't care less what hour
            of the day or night it is.

SHIRLEY   (*almost in tears*) You're unbelievable, you
            really are!

ARTHUR   (*rising*) Look here, young lady . . .

MARY   (*restraining him*) Arthur, not now . . .

SHIRLEY   We're seventeen, Dad! By that age you were
            earning your own living, and dating half the girls
            in Essex. You've told us so yourself.

ARTHUR   That's different - I was a feller . . .

SHIRLEY   Oh Christ!

ARTHUR   . . . so I know what they're after.

SHIRLEY   You don't have to judge everyone else by your
            own standards.

ARTHUR   Now look . . .

MARY   Oh, don't make such a scene about it, Arthur.
            They'll be all right. (*Grimaces desperately, and
            gestures at* JOHN *and* CAROL.)

ARTHUR   (*deflating somewhat*) Well, I don't know. I'm at
            my wit's end. What do you say about it, John?

JOHN   I honestly think they'll be all right. Wendy's
            very responsible.

SHIRLEY   *I'm* very responsible!

JOHN   Oh yes, I didn't mean to . . .

SHIRLEY   Anyone would think I was twelve years old, and
            a convicted child prostitute and dope addict!

MARY   Oh, Shirley . . .

SHIRLEY   I mean what's everyone afraid of?

ARTHUR   (*looking at his watch*) One hour, and that's my
            last word. Back here by ten thirty, or there'll be
            real trouble. Understand?

SHIRLEY   Ever thought of getting a job as a prison warden,
            Dad? You'd be very good. Come on, Wendy.

WENDY   (*kissing her mother*) We won't be long, Mummy.

CAROL   Do be careful, darling.

WENDY   Of course we will. (*Kisses her father*.) 'Bye,
            Daddy.

SHIRLEY   (*muttering*) You'd think we were leaving for the
            South Pole.

            (*They go off.* ARTHUR *brings brandy for* JOHN *and*
            CAROL. MARY *goes back to the washing up.*)

ARTHUR   Kids today. I don't know.

SHIRLEY   (*as she and* WENDY *cross the gangplank*) I'll kill
            that man one of these days. I will. I'll push him
            under a bus!

CAROL   (*as* ARTHUR *holds out the brandy glass*) You
             don't by any chance have any um . . . Bailey's,
             or anything like that, do you?

ARTHUR   Don't know. I'll have a look.

WENDY   (*on the river bank*) Do you think they'll be
             there?

SHIRLEY   Who?

WENDY   Those two boys. At the disco.

SHIRLEY   'Course they will. They fancied us rotten.

WENDY   I'm not sure I fancied them much.

SHIRLEY   Well there'll be plenty of others. Come on. We
             said we'd be there an hour ago.

             (*They go off.* ARTHUR *is searching among the
             bottles.*)

ARTHUR   I know it's a cliche to go on about one's
             offspring, but I think something's gone very
             wrong with today's bunch. What do you say,
             John?

JOHN   Well, in all honesty . . .

ARTHUR   I mean, if I'd talked to my father the way Shirley
             talks to me, I'd have had a sore arse for days!
             I've got some Tia Maria, Carol. Will that do?

CAROL   Lovely. Just a small one though.

ARTHUR   I tell you, John, it's the things they see on telly.

JOHN   Well, that's perhaps a little . . .

ARTHUR   It's all these trashy American programmes. All
             these so-called liberal attitudes. Anyone can do
             anything with a credit card, a gun, and a
             condom. The Yanks have got a lot to answer for,
             you know.

JOHN	Mm . . .
ARTHUR	The Yanks and the socialists.
	(*Hands* CAROL *her drink*.)
	How's that?
CAROL	Golly - rather a big one.
ARTHUR	Well, you're a big girl.
CAROL	Lovely - thank you.
ARTHUR	(*irritably*) Mary, don't do the washing up now! Come and join us.
MARY	It won't take long. I like to get it done.
CAROL	(*rising*) Oh, I'll give you a hand, Mary.
ARTHUR	(*almost pushing her down again*) No, you won't. You stay there.
CAROL	Oh.
ARTHUR	Mary, I said leave it.
MARY	Well, I was just . . .
ARTHUR	I can't stand clinking and clattering while we're trying to have our coffee! I've told you before - the meal's not over till the last brandy's been drunk.
MARY	I'm sorry, I just like to get it done - then I can relax.
ARTHUR	(*handing a brandy glass to* MARY) Here.
	(MARY *pulls up a chair, and sits.* ARTHUR *pours himself a drink.*)

ARTHUR   I'll tell you something else, John, it's the new
          methods of education as much as anything. Cut
          out discipline, cut out competition, cut out hard
          work. I tell you, I can understand why so many
          people are turning to the private education
          system, can't you?

JOHN   Well, I . . .

ARTHUR   I'd have done it myself, if I didn't resent paying
          out all that money when I'm already paying
          enough taxes to run an entire comprehensive
          school on my own. More brandy?

JOHN   Er . . . no, thanks. I've hardly started this.

          (ARTHUR *pours him some anyway.*)

ARTHUR   I've been meaning to talk to you about this,
          John.

JOHN   About what?

ARTHUR   Schools. I mean look at Collier's School, where
          our two go. It's a shambles!

JOHN   Is it? We've found it rather good actually.

ARTHUR   I mean, half the pupils are out playing truant
          most of the time; the other half are into drink,
          and drugs, and getting themselves pregnant
          behind the sports pavilion!

JOHN   Well, there are a few miscreants as in any
          school, but I think in all honesty they set a pretty
          good standard.

ARTHUR   Huh! Well I wish I did. The way Shirley has
          changed in the last year or two hasn't been a
          pretty sight, and I put it all down to the influence
          of that school.

CAROL   Oh, but she's a nice girl - Shirley.

ARTHUR   (*scarcely hearing*) I think the sooner they carry
            out this plan to merge it with St Ronan's the
            better. What do you think?

JOHN   Ah, well that's a different matter. I'm not
            honestly sure about that.

ARTHUR   Makes such sense though, doesn't it? What with
            falling numbers, there isn't room for two
            comprehensives in our area now. It's the perfect
            opportunity to put them together, and shake up
            the system at the same time.

JOHN   Well . . .

ARTHUR   I mean, you're Chairman of the P.T.A. What's
            the general feeling about it?

JOHN   There's a lot of resistance. From both parents
            and teachers.

ARTHUR   Well there's always resistance to progress, isn't
            there? But it makes sense - one good school,
            instead of two mediocre ones . . .

JOHN   Ah, but . . .

ARTHUR   . . . and above all, it releases the most valuable
            site in the town for development.

JOHN   Ah, yes - now we're coming to it.

ARTHUR   Eh? What do you mean?

JOHN   That's what you're honestly interested in, isn't
            it?

ARTHUR   Well of course I am. I am, after all, a developer.
            But with the town's interests at heart, John.
            First and foremost always the town's interests at
            heart.

JOHN   Of course.

ARTHUR   And you're the key to the whole enterprise, John.
           You hold the success or failure of the entire
           caboodle in your hands.

JOHN   I'd hardly say that.

ARTHUR   Oh, come on now. Let's not beat about the bush.
           Let's talk straight.

           (*Opens a box of cigars and offers* JOHN *one.*)

           Cigar? (JOHN *declines.*) You're a governor of
           Collier's, and chairman of the Parent Teachers
           Association. And if they come down on the side
           of the merger, then that's half the battle.
           There'll be no whining from those petty
           bureaucrats at the Education Authority about not
           having the support of local opinion. There'll be
           no threats about appealing to the Education
           Minister.

JOHN   Well . . .

           (ARTHUR *lights a match and holds it out for the
           cigar* JOHN *hasn't taken.*)

           No, thank you.

ARTHUR   (*lighting his own cigar*) And secondly - and
           even more important - you're also chairman of
           the council planning committee. Which of
           course has to pass the scheme for a supermarket
           on the Collier's site. And that, as I'm sure you
           realise, is the financial key to the whole thing.

JOHN   Just because I'm chairman, doesn't mean that I
           can dictate decisions.

ARTHUR   Of course not, but it means you've got a hell of a
           lot of influence over them, eh? Ha, ha.
           (*Warming to his theme in increasingly drunken
           fashion.*) Now look, John. I believe in putting
           cards on the table in a discussion like this.
           Don't you?

JOHN   Of course.

ARTHUR   Now you and I, in our different ways, are two of
              the most powerful men in our town.

JOHN   Well, I . . .

ARTHUR   Yes, we are - let's be honest about it. You've
              got where you are by hard work, and integrity,
              and acclip . . . ap . . . application. Hasn't he,
              Carol?

CAROL   Yes, he has. He's a very dedicated . . .

ARTHUR   (*charging on*) And I've got there by hard work,
              and know-how, and seeing the opportunities . . .

MARY   And integrity too, Arthur.

ARTHUR   Don't interrupt, Mary . . . Oh, yes - integrity too
              of course, that goes without saying. Now the
              town needs men of vision like us. There are
              precious too few around - particularly amongst
              that bunch of prats on the council.

MARY   (*warningly*) Arthur . . .

ARTHUR   The point is this. That schools merger, and the
              development of the Collier's site is the most
              important opportunity that's appeared in the
              town for years . . . decades!

JOHN   One of them, certainly.

ARTHUR   And I put it to you, John, that the thing the town
              needs above everything else at this point in its
              history is a good supermarket. Modern facility
              for the smart new generation we're trying to
              attract. Get all those shoppers' cars and delivery
              lorries out of the High Street . . .

JOHN   There's a lot of opposition from the small shop-
              keepers.

ARTHUR   John, progress always has to be pushed through
              against the small man. But in the end it's him
              who benefits. Without it he dies.

JOHN   Well, that's honestly a bit . . .

ARTHUR   Now the point is this . . . Mary, where are the
              After Eights?

MARY   Bread bin.

ARTHUR   Naturally. (*Goes to get them, talking as he
              goes.*) I've got Garrett's dangling on a string
              over that site. They've been wanting to get into
              the town for years, and that's the only spot that
              gives them everything they need - location,
              access, car parking . . .

JOHN   There's the Old Market.

ARTHUR   (*offering him the After Eights*) Would the
              planning committee allow that?

JOHN   Well I haven't said so, but . . .

              (*As he goes to take an After Eight,* ARTHUR *moves
              on.*)

ARTHUR   'Course they wouldn't. Cause an outcry - local
              landmark like that. Besides, there's too many
              problems - wrong size and shape, poor position,
              tricky access . . . (*Puts the After Eights on the
              table.*) No, it's the Collier's site Garrett's want.
              It's a chance that may not come their way again.
              And we can't afford to lose them.

JOHN   Yes, but there are other considerations . . .

ARTHUR   Of course there are, but it's a question of
              priorities, John. This is a chance to put both the
              town's education *and* shopping facilities right in
              one fell sweep . . . or is it swoop? And you and
              I can achieve that together. How's your brandy?

JOHN   I've had enough, honestly.

(ARTHUR *pours him some more, then takes*
CAROL'S *glass to replenish it.*)

ARTHUR   A drop more of that, Carol. You look as if you
          need it.

CAROL   Just a tiny one, really.

JOHN   And of course there are other contenders for the
          supermarket idea besides Garrett's.

ARTHUR   I know, I know. Thames Stores want to get their
          dirty toes in as well. But I ask you, John - do we
          really want Jack Craddock moving in? I mean
          do we really want that jumped-up barrow-boy on
          our patch?

JOHN   He runs a very slick operation.

MARY   I like his shops. Don't you, Carol?

CAROL   Yes, they're always very pleasant to . . .

ARTHUR   (*with a murderous glance at* MARY) Slick - that's
          the word exactly. They're just flashy showplaces
          designed to fool the housewife into paying more
          for her groceries.

CAROL   Oh no, things are usually a bit cheaper at Thames
          Stores, I find. Don't you, Mary?

MARY   Oh yes, on the whole . . .

ARTHUR   Loss-leaders! Oldest trick in the book. Clever
          use of loss-leaders to con the customer. But . . .

JOHN   He's making a strong play for the contract.

ARTHUR   Of course he is. He knows what it's worth. But
          . . . he hasn't got to you, has he, John?

JOHN   Got to me?

ARTHUR   I mean, er . . . he hasn't made you an offer of
            any sort?

JOHN   Me? You mean the council?

ARTHUR   No. I mean you personally.

JOHN   No, of course not.

ARTHUR   Ah.

JOHN   But he has made approaches to the council as a
            body.

ARTHUR   Oh yes, of course he has. You bet he has. And
            what do they think of him - as a body?

JOHN   Well, to tell you the truth, most of the
            councillors are against his ultra-modern style of
            store.

ARTHUR   Ah.

JOHN   They want something more traditional, more . . .

ARTHUR   Conservative.

JOHN   Yes.

ARTHUR   Can't say I blame them. And do you agree with
            them?

JOHN   Well I reserve judgement. It's my job to reflect
            the general opinion.

ARTHUR   You have a casting vote, don't you?

JOHN   Ah, but only in the case of an impasse. And I
            hope it would never come to that.

ARTHUR   Yes. (*His tone changes.*) You see . . . the great
            thing about a project as big as this, John, is that
            there's so much capital involved no one need be
            out of pocket over it. Know what I mean?

JOHN   No - not really.

ARTHUR   Well, what I mean is that with a project like this
          . . . I mean the size of this, there's enough profit
          involved to benefit all parties. The schools, the
          Education Authority, the council . . . and the
          individuals who've put their time and expertise
          into getting the whole thing off the ground.

JOHN   Oh, I wouldn't want payment. I sit on my
          various committees and so forth voluntarily.

ARTHUR   Of course you do, John. That goes without
          saying. But nevertheless it's only fair that all
          the hard work a man like you puts into the
          community should occasionally get something
          out of it. I'm not talking about . . . well,
          payment as such.

JOHN   What are you talking about?

ARTHUR   I'm talking about . . . recognition. A gesture of
          gratitude from the consortium that's benefitting
          from your contribution - that's all.

JOHN   I haven't said I'm going to contribute yet.

ARTHUR   No, I know you haven't. But if you did, then . . .

JOHN   I'm not honestly sure what you're saying, Arthur.

ARTHUR   Well, let me put it this way . . . Er - John needs
          some more coffee, Mary.

JOHN   No, I'm fine, thanks.

MARY   I'll get some anyway. (*Busies herself.*)

ARTHUR   Do you have your own holiday place, Carol?

CAROL   Holiday place?

ARTHUR   Yes - you know . . . little cottage somewhere, a
          timeshare perhaps . . .

CAROL	Oh, no we don't. Can't afford it for one thing, and we've never . . .
ARTHUR	It's a marvellous thing to have your own bolt-hole, you know. Somewhere to escape to, hide from the pressures of the world . . .
CAROL	Yes, it must be.
ARTHUR	For instance - take this boat. It's a joy to own something like this.
CAROL	I can imagine.
ARTHUR	Gives an added dimension to life. How would you like to?
CAROL	What?
ARTHUR	Own something like this.
CAROL	This boat?
ARTHUR	Yes.
JOHN	This boat?
ARTHUR	Yes. Somewhere to escape to for the weekends. For you as a family to relax and enjoy yourselves.
JOHN	Well, we'd love it of course, but . . .
ARTHUR	You see, the point is this, John. This boat technically belongs to my company. It was bought to use for extra office space, entertaining clients - as I'm entertaining you now, ha, ha - and so forth. And as such it's a depreciating asset - hardly any sale value on the books now.
CAROL	You wouldn't want to sell it, would you?
ARTHUR	No, no, of course we wouldn't, Carol. But what I'm getting at is that there'd be nothing

whatsoever against my company making a little gift of something like this, in recognition of your husband's services. See what I mean?

(*Pause.*)

JOHN   This boat?

ARTHUR   Yes.

CAROL   The Bunty?

ARTHUR   Yes.

MARY   Oh, Arthur . . .

(*He gestures at her.*)

JOHN   Let me get this straight. This project is worth so much to you that it's worth your while using something as valuable as this boat . . .

ARTHUR   Not valuable, John. Not to my company, as I've explained.

JOHN   Well then - as *big* as this boat - to bribe someone . . .

ARTHUR   Now that's unfair. I never said bribe, John. It's a gift, a reward.

JOHN   To reward someone for getting the scheme through for you.

ARTHUR   Yes, that's right. And no one need know. It's a disposable asset. We'll put it in whatever name you like - Carol's perhaps. And you can tell your friends you picked it up cheap. All perfectly legal, and what's more - just.

JOHN   Just.

ARTHUR   Yes. A just reward.

(*Silence. They all watch* JOHN, *who sits expressionless.*)

JOHN	I don't know what to say.
ARTHUR	Don't say anything just now.
JOHN	I'm flabbergasted.
ARTHUR	Just think about it over the weekend. There's no hurry.
JOHN	It's the most outrageous thing I've ever heard.
ARTHUR	Oh, nonsense, John. It's normal business practice. It happens all the time.
JOHN	Not in my experience.
ARTHUR	No, well you're moving into the big time now, John. When there's many millions involved, like now, people make these little arrangements to oil the wheels - cut through all the red tape. It's perfectly standard practice, I promise you.
JOHN	(*rising*) Excuse me. I think I need the toilet.
MARY	You've got your own, next to your . . .
JOHN	Yes, I know. Thank you.
	(*He goes off to his cabin, from where he goes into the shower room. There is a slightly awkward silence in the saloon.*)
ARTHUR	How's your drink, Carol?
CAROL	It's fine, thank you. Full.
ARTHUR	I hope John understands that I'm not asking him to do anything underhand.
CAROL	Oh, yes.
ARTHUR	Simply use his influence for the good of the town.
CAROL	Of course.

ARTHUR   I just don't believe such things should go unrewarded. D'you understand?

CAROL   Absolutely.

ARTHUR   Good.

     (*Pause.*)

CAROL   (*rising*) I think I'd better just see if he's all right.

     (*Goes next door. Taps on the shower room door.*)

     John? Are you all right?

     (*Silence. She sits on the bed. Next door, MARY has started clearing the coffee cups. There is a strained silence between them as she bangs crockery about.*)

ARTHUR   (*eventually*) All right, what is it?

MARY   You never even discussed it. You never even mentioned it to me.

ARTHUR   It's business.

MARY   (*quivering with emotion*) It's our boat. The Bunty is ours. It belongs to the family.

ARTHUR   You don't even like it.

MARY   Of course we like it. We love it!

ARTHUR   Shirley can't wait to get off it. And you get into such a state about coming down here, it's hardly worth doing.

MARY   That's only because you make it all so difficult. Giving orders right, left and centre as if you were running a destroyer at the Falklands . . . We'd all love it here if you'd just let us. But

now you're going to give it away as a bribe to
that . . .

ARTHUR   It's not a bribe, Mary! Don't you ever call it a
bribe! It's a perfectly legal business
arrangement.

MARY   I don't care what you call it - you should have
discussed it with us first. It's our boat as much
as yours.

ARTHUR   We can get another one. Boats are ten a penny.

MARY   What, and go through all that hell of getting it
done up again? With you shouting and
screaming at everyone because it's not done the
way you want it, and Shirley and me in tears, and
workmen walking off the job, and . . .

ARTHUR   I can't help being a perfectionist, can I?

MARY   Perfectionist? You're a blooming madman over
something like this! You're . . .

ARTHUR   (*trying to placate her*) Anyway, love, if we can
pull off this deal, we'll be able to afford a *real*
boat.

MARY   What do you mean, a real boat?

ARTHUR   A proper sailing boat. A sea-going boat.

MARY   Sea-going?

ARTHUR   Yes. Remember how we used to look at the
boats down at Lymington, or in France?
Remember how we dreamt of having one one
day?

MARY   That was just fantasies. We weren't serious.

ARTHUR   I was. Why do you think I get all these sailing
books and magazines?

MARY   I thought you were just playing at it.

ARTHUR   I've always wanted a real boat.

MARY   Then why d'you buy 'The Bunty'?

ARTHUR   It was the next best thing. I never had the time
                or the money for a yacht. But soon we could
                have the time *and* the money. Just think of it,
                Mary. A real sailing boat. Not too big. Just
                something we can take across the Channel -
                perhaps eventually sail to the Med.

MARY   You don't know how to sail one of those things.

ARTHUR   I know more than you think. And you'd get the
                hang of it in no time.

                (*Next door,* JOHN *comes out of the shower room,
                and sits on the bed beside* CAROL. *She puts her
                arms round him, and starts stroking his head and
                kissing his neck. He shows no response.*)

MARY   I don't want to get the hang of it. I like the
                Bunty. It's cosy and not too swanky, and I like
                it. (*Close to tears.*) And now you've given it
                away!

ARTHUR   Look, it's still just a suggestion - a bargaining
                point to start the negotiations going. We may
                end up paying him a direct commission in the
                end.

MARY   Never! Not him. He's a solicitor. He's a man
                of integrity. You couldn't . . .

ARTHUR   Don't kid yourself, Mary. He's a man like any
                other man. Have you noticed how often he uses
                the word honesty in his conversation?

MARY   No.

ARTHUR   All the time. (*Mimics* JOHN.) 'In all honesty . . .
                I honestly think . . . to be quite honest . . . '

MARY   So what?

ARTHUR   Never trust a man who talks like that. I tell you,
            as long as I don't ask him to actually *do* anything
            illegal, he'll go for it in the end. He won't let an
            opportunity like this slip by.

MARY   I think that's a dreadful suggestion! They're an
            honourable family. They've got a very respected
            name in the town . . .

ARTHUR   Who says?

MARY   *I* say. Shirley's told me all about them. They do
            things for charity, and belong to the bridge club,
            and watch 'Songs Of Praise' on television . . .

ARTHUR   God help us!

MARY   (*the flood gates open, and she fishes for a
            handkerchief*) Well, I don't care, I wish we were
            like them! I wish we had a nice, loving,
            respectable family life like they do. I'd give all
            the blooming boats in the world for that!

ARTHUR   (*banging a bottle down on the table*) All right!
            All right, we'll talk about it! Just don't start
            weeping and wailing all over the place, that's
            all. They think we're loony enough as it is. Let
            them see you in one of your hysterias, and
            they'll be running for home faster than you can
            say "Man the lifeboats!"

MARY   Well, I can't help it! You make me like this.
            (*Blows her nose loudly.*) And give me some
            more of that brandy. On top of it all, you're
            stingy as well!

            (*He raises his eyes to the heavens in
            hopelessness. Next door, under* CAROL'S
            administrations, JOHN *pulls himself out of his
            stupor.*)

JOHN   What ever persuaded us to come on this wretched
            weekend?

CAROL   I'm quite enjoying it in a funny sort of way.

JOHN   You are?

CAROL   Well, he's an odd sort of man, but if you don't take him too seriously . . .

JOHN   How can you not take that sort of suggestion seriously? It's out and out bribery! I've honestly never met such an outrageous approach before in my life. (*Pause.*) The funny thing is, he probably doesn't even need to go to those lengths.

CAROL   Why?

JOHN   He's more-or-less got it in the bag, although he doesn't know it.

CAROL   What do you mean?

JOHN   Well, it's almost certain that the Garrett's plan will go through anyway. The decision on the schools is virtually irrevocable now, though the opposition are refusing to admit it - and Jack Craddock is probably out of the running for the supermarket contract, because none of the planning committee wants one of his space-age buildings in the town. So Bullhead's almost home and dry.

          (*Pause.*)

CAROL   Really?

JOHN   Yes.

CAROL   So if he's got it anyway . . . I mean, if you don't actually have to pull any strings . . . then there'd be no harm.

JOHN   In what?

CAROL   Us accepting the boat.

(*He stares at her.*)

JOHN   Carol!

(*The lights fade.*)

Scene Three

*The same, an hour or so later. Fade up on both the saloon
and the guest cabin. The lights are low in both.* CAROL *is
sitting disconsolately on the bed in the cabin, staring at the
floor.* ARTHUR *is in the saloon, pouring himself a brandy.
There is no sign of the other two.* ARTHUR *lights a cigar, then
takes it and his brandy out onto the fore-deck, turning off the
lights in the saloon as he goes. He stands in the semi-
darkness for a few moments, peering off along the river bank.
Then he climbs up onto the roof, sits down on a sun mattress,
and makes himself comfortable there, gazing out across the
river.*

CAROL *sighs, rises, looks unhappily at the shower room door,
then goes out of the cabin and into the saloon. She stumbles
awkwardly across it in the darkness, bumping into the
furniture, and muttering to herself. She finally makes it to
the door and clambers up the steps onto the fore-deck, where
she stands uncertainly peering about her.* ARTHUR *hears her
coming, and peers down from the roof.*

ARTHUR   Who's that?

CAROL   (*jumping*) Oh!

ARTHUR   Hello. Is that you?

CAROL   Sorry, you startled me. I didn't know anyone
            was out here.

ARTHUR   Just taking a breath of night air. I didn't feel
            like turning in just yet.

CAROL   Me neither.

ARTHUR   Where's John?

CAROL   Getting ready for bed. He's an early-to-bed,
           early-to-rise sort.

ARTHUR   Ah. Mary's gone to bed too. Sulking.

CAROL   Sulking?

ARTHUR   Bit off me at the moment.

CAROL   Oh dear.

ARTHUR   Don't worry. She'll be all right in the morning.

CAROL   Ah.

ARTHUR   Want to come up here?

CAROL   Oh, well . . . it looks a bit tricky.

ARTHUR   Only if you've got a tight skirt on - ha, ha. I'll
           give you a hand.

           (*He reaches down and helps her climb up.*)

           Only a sun mattress to sit on I'm afraid.

CAROL   (*sitting beside him*) That's fine.

ARTHUR   Like a brandy? I could get the bottle.

CAROL   Heavens - no, thank you! I'm already not sure
           whether it's the boat rocking, or me.

ARTHUR   Ah.

CAROL   Lovely night.

ARTHUR   Yes. I love the night time.

CAROL   Do you?

ARTHUR   On the river, I do.

CAROL   Yes, it's beautiful.

ARTHUR   You could be on the Nile. Amazon even. Deep
            in the jungle - only the beasts of the night to see
            you.

CAROL   I hope there are no beasts here.

ARTHUR   Oh, you'd be surprised what beasts there are
            around Pangbourne-on-Thames. Look out!

            (*She jumps and squeals. He puts an arm round
            her, and laughs.*)

            Had you there.

CAROL   Oh, you pig!

ARTHUR   Talking of beasts - where are those girls? They
            should have been back half an hour ago. I'll
            murder that daughter of mine one of these days.

CAROL   Oh, they're only young once.

ARTHUR   Well I wish they'd remember just how young
            they are. Shirley behaves as if she's free to do
            any damn thing she wants.

            (JOHN *comes out of the shower room below,
            wearing pyjamas. He sees the cabin is empty,
            stands uncertainly for a moment, then gets into
            bed.*)

CAROL   What is Mary upset about?

ARTHUR   Mary?

CAROL   You said she was cross with you.

ARTHUR   Oh, yes, well . . . It's just a mood. She gets
            cross with me when I have too much of this stuff.

CAROL   Ah.

ARTHUR   I don't suppose you have that problem with John.

CAROL   No, he hardly ever drinks too much.

ARTHUR   I thought not.

CAROL   And when he does have a bit over the top - like
            tonight - he still manages to stay utterly calm
            and utterly reasonable. He's amazing.

ARTHUR   (*non-committal*) Yes.

CAROL   I admire him so much. D'you know, I've never
            known him lose his temper. Ever.

ARTHUR   Never?

CAROL   Never, ever.

ARTHUR   Amazing.

CAROL   I've never even known him get rattled. He
            always retains his self-control and reasonable . . .
            ness. He's just wonderful.

ARTHUR   What a lucky girl you are.

CAROL   (*nodding*) I'm sometimes amazed at how lucky I
            am. A lovely husband. A lovely daughter. I'm
            one of the luckiest people alive.

ARTHUR   And they're lucky too - having lovely you.

CAROL   Ah, well I'm not so sure about that.

ARTHUR   Oh, yes. You're the loveliest of the lot.
            Especially when your shirt is open at the top like
            that.

CAROL   (*giggling*) That's naughty! (*She pulls her shirt
            together, but doesn't do it up.*) That's not what
            I'm talking about - and you know it.

ARTHUR   Oh, and you're lovely in the other ways too, of
            course. In fact you're a very lovely family
            altogether. That's one of the reasons Mary was
            getting upset tonight.

CAROL   Why?

ARTHUR   Jealous. Why can't we be as lovely a family as
            you are, she wanted to know.

CAROL   Oh, but you are!

ARTHUR   Oh no. Not like you. We have rows, and make
            balls-ups, and get ourselves into right-old
            messes. And it's usually my fault when it comes
            down to it. No, she'd really like to be like you.
            Ideal husband, well-behaved daughter,
            everything straight out of the magazines.

CAROL   You make us sound awful!

ARTHUR   Why?

CAROL   We're not *that* perfect. I mean we don't always
            do things right.

ARTHUR   Yes, you do. Look at old John. As you said
            yourself, never puts a foot wrong. Wouldn't be
            surprised if they don't canonise him eventually.
            Saint John the Honest. Statue of him in Civic
            Square with little wings on the back.

CAROL   (*giggling*) Oh, that's awful! Even John makes
            mistakes, you know.

ARTHUR   When? When did he ever make a mistake?

CAROL   You'd be surprised. He's human after all.

ARTHUR   Oh good, I'm glad to hear that.

CAROL   He once even came near to getting struck off as a
            solicitor.

ARTHUR   You're kidding. John?

CAROL   It wasn't really his fault.

ARTHUR   There you are - of course it wasn't.

CAROL   But he got himself into a nasty corner all the
            same. He still has nightmares about it.

ARTHUR   What happened?

CAROL   He used some of the money in his client's
            account to get himself out of trouble. Something
            a solicitor *never* does.

ARTHUR   Really?

CAROL   It was several years ago now. He was in a
            dreadful spot. Lost a couple of large corporate
            accounts, which were his bread-and-butter, and
            suddenly found himself in real trouble. Hadn't
            got enough to pay the rent on the premises, his
            staff's salaries - even our mortgage.

ARTHUR   Oh dear.

CAROL   It was only temporary - he knew he had more
            work coming up - but the bank wouldn't lend
            him any more, and he had to do something fast,
            otherwise the whole practice might have
            collapsed.

ARTHUR   So he raided the clients' account?

CAROL   Only borrowed. But it was a dreadful thing for a
            lawyer to do.

ARTHUR   Yes.

CAROL   He went through agonies of doubt, but it was
            either that or go under. And then, to make
            matters worse, he nearly got caught.

ARTHUR   How?

CAROL   Well, he calculated that it would only be for a
            week or two at the most. But then one of his
            clients, who'd paid quite a lot of money into the
            account prior to the completion of some property
            deal, suddenly decided he wanted to hurry the

deal forward and complete very urgently. Well,
there wasn't enough left in to do it, and John had
to hold him off with stories about technical
difficulties and legal problems, and so on. It was
a terrible time.

ARTHUR   What happened?

CAROL   He eventually scraped home by the skin of his
teeth, but he'd had to hold up the deal by a
couple of weeks. The client wasn't able to
organise his building schedule as he'd wanted,
and in the end it cost him several thousand.

ARTHUR   Did it?

CAROL   He was a very rich man anyway, so it didn't
matter too much, but John felt dreadful about it.
Didn't sleep for weeks.

ARTHUR   Dear, oh dear.

CAROL   In fact he nearly had a breakdown. He takes
things like that terribly seriously.

ARTHUR   Who was the client? Would I know him?

CAROL   Yes, as a matter of fact you would.

ARTHUR   Really?

CAROL   It was your old friend, Jack Craddock.

ARTHUR   No!

CAROL   It was before he founded Thames Stores as a
public company. This was his own personal
project. A petrol station or something.

ARTHUR   (*reflectively*) A petrol station.

CAROL   He was very keen to get it built quickly for some
reason, so he was livid about the hold-up.
Fortunately he never found out what had really
happened.

ARTHUR   Well, well . . .

CAROL   So you see, even John has feet of clay, or
          Achilles heels, or whatever you call it. (*Pause.*)
          I think I would like a sip of brandy after all.

ARTHUR   (*passing it to her*) Here.

          (*She sips at it. He watches her.*)

          John's a very lucky man, having you.

CAROL   (*coy*) Are you being flirty?

ARTHUR   Yes.

CAROL   If I wasn't so drunk, I'd be cross.

ARTHUR   But you aren't.

CAROL   Well, it's nice to be . . .

ARTHUR   Desired?

CAROL   Yes.

ARTHUR   In vino veritas.

CAROL   What do you mean by that?

ARTHUR   That's your true feelings. You'd only be cross
          because it was expected of you.

CAROL   That's not true. I'm not a promiscuous sort of
          girl.

ARTHUR   Of course you're not. But you're passionate.
          Admit it.

CAROL   Well, yes, I am . . . quite. But I've never been
          unfaithful to John. Never.

ARTHUR   Never?

CAROL   Never, ever.

ARTHUR   But that doesn't mean you haven't wanted to,
           does it? It's only natural - for a passionate
           person. Shall I tell you something?

CAROL   What?

ARTHUR   Promise you won't be cross?

CAROL   Well I won't know that until I hear what it is.

ARTHUR   One of the reasons I invited you all to come here
           this weekend was because of you.

CAROL   Me?

ARTHUR   Yes.

CAROL   What do you mean?

ARTHUR   I've always watched you from a distance, and
           thought, 'There's an attractive woman. That's
           the sort of woman I could really fall for.' Not
           with any real hopes of anything coming from it,
           you understand. You're a truly faithful woman -
           I can tell that. But that's part of the attraction.

CAROL   You've got a lovely wife.

ARTHUR   Oh yes. But just because you've got a bunch of
           daisies doesn't mean you don't hanker after roses
           too - ha. ha.

CAROL   I take it that was an attempt at being poetic.

ARTHUR   I may not be poetic, but I am romantic
           underneath. After all, romance is what keeps the
           spark in life, isn't it?

CAROL   Yes.

ARTHUR   And you must admit, however much you need
           marriage, it's jolly hard to keep romance going
           in it.

CAROL   I suppose it is.

(*He puts a hand inside her dress. She gives a little gasp, and then sighs.*)

ARTHUR   That's lovely.

(*She sighs again.*)

That's beautiful.

CAROL   I mustn't . . . We can't . . .

ARTHUR   Of course not. But we can pretend.

(*He kisses her, his hand still inside her dress. She succumbs, and they sink slowly back onto the mattress. It is getting fairly steamy, when there is the sound of voices from the river bank. They freeze.*)

SHIRLEY   . . . look, for God's sake, calm down! You can't go back in this state. You'll wake up the whole boat.

WENDY   (*wailing*) What am I going to do? What am I going to tell them? They'll never forgive me - never, never!

SHIRLEY   Don't tell them. Just keep quiet about it. It's not the end of the world.

WENDY   But they'll know. They'll know I'm upset, and they'll want to know why.

SHIRLEY   Well make up some other reason. Look, for heaven's sake, Wendy, you're seventeen after all. It's only your virginity - not a nuclear holocaust.

CAROL   (*from the roof*) Oh . . . !

ARTHUR   Shhhh!

SHIRLEY   I mean, if I'd known you were still a virgin, I'd never have suggested we went off with them.

WENDY	I might be pregnant. I might have caught something!
SHIRLEY	Of course you haven't. Didn't he use anything?
WENDY	I don't think so. How do you know?
SHIRLEY	Well you'd have seen him put it on! They don't go around wearing them like spare socks, you know.
WENDY	No. Oh God! Oh God, help me! What am I going to do?
SHIRLEY	Stop snivelling and get on board for a start. (*Starts to cross the gangplank.*) We ought to be celebrating. It's a big occasion - your first feller.
ARTHUR	(*rising like the wrath of God*) Celebrating! I'll give you celebrating, young woman!
SHIRLEY	Oh, my God!
ARTHUR	What the bloody hell have you been up to?
WENDY	(*wailing on the bank*) Ohhhh!
CAROL	Wendy, darling . . .
WENDY	Oh, Mummy . . .
ARTHUR	What the blazes have you gone and done now? Eh?
SHIRLEY	Nothing, Dad . . .
ARTHUR	Nothing? Nothing? It sounds as if you've been to a bloody orgy with half the yobs in town!
WENDY	Oh, Mummy, Mummy . . . !
CAROL	(*hurrying down the ladder to her*) Wendy, darling, it's all right.

(*Down below, the cabin light comes on, and* JOHN *sits up in bed, listening to the noise.*)

ARTHUR   Just look at her! She looks as if she's been assaulted by a platoon of marines in a hay field.

SHIRLEY   Don't be ridiculous!

ARTHUR   And you don't look any better. Christ, I'll swing for you! I swear, one of these days I'll swing for you!

(WENDY *is now weeping in* CAROL'S *arms on the river bank.* SHIRLEY *is on the fore-deck. The saloon lights come on, and* MARY *appears from the corridor, pulling on a gown over her nightdress.* JOHN *gets out of bed, and leaves the cabin.*)

CAROL   What happened, darling? What happened?

WENDY   (*through her tears*) We went to a dance.

CAROL   Dance?

WENDY   There was a disco on at the village hall. And we met these boys there.

ARTHUR   Boys? What boys? Not that couple of morons down at the pub?

SHIRLEY   Just boys, Dad.

ARTHUR   It was those two, wasn't it? It was those two from the pub?

SHIRLEY   Well, what if it was? They're human, just like any others.

ARTHUR   Yes, they sound human! They sound as if they've proved just how bloody human they are in no uncertain manner!

WENDY   Ohhhhh!

SHIRLEY   Well we're all human, Dad. You too, by the
            looks of things.

ARTHUR   What?

SHIRLEY   What were you doing up there, lying around on
            the sun mattress at midnight? Sunbathing?

ARTHUR   My God! I'll . . .

            (*As he goes for the ladder, the saloon door
            opens, and* MARY *comes out.* JOHN *is crossing the
            saloon behind her.*)

MARY   What's going on? What's happened? What's all
            the noise about?

SHIRLEY   (*turning away in exasperation*) Oh, Christ!

ARTHUR   (*still on the roof*) You may well ask, Mary!
            'They'll be all right', you said. 'We can trust
            them to be responsible', you said.

MARY   What's *happened*?

ARTHUR   They've been responsible all right - for getting
            Wendy knocked up by the sound of it!

WENDY   (*hysterical*) Ohhhhh!

CAROL   It's all right, darling. Don't get upset.

JOHN   (*appearing from the saloon*) What's happened?
            What is it?

ARTHUR   Here we go. (*To* SHIRLEY.) Go on - you explain.
            You got us into this. You tell him!

            (JOHN *joins* MARY *and* SHIRLEY *on the fore-deck.*)

JOHN   Explain what?

ARTHUR   Go on, tell him!

SHIRLEY   (*defiant*) I'm not telling him anything. It wasn't
               my fault.

JOHN   Tell me what?

SHIRLEY   I'm not her nanny!

JOHN   (*pushing past* MARY *to the gangplank*) For God's
               sake, Carol, what's happened?

CAROL   (*with* WENDY *at the other end of the gangplank*)
               I'll tell you later, John.

JOHN   (*furiously*) I want to know now!

ARTHUR   (*starting to climb down from the roof*) It's all
               right, John. Nothing to get too upset about.
               Let's all go back inside.

MARY   Don't you come down, Arthur - there isn't room.

ARTHUR   The whole bloody river's listening to us. Let's
               talk about it inside, everyone. (*To* SHIRLEY.)
               That means you too, young woman!

               (*He reaches the deck, as* CAROL *urges* WENDY *to
               cross the gangplank in front of her.*)

CAROL   Go on, darling.

SHIRLEY   You go inside. I'm not talking about it to
               anyone.

               (*She is on one side of* MARY *and* JOHN, *nearest
               the bows -* ARTHUR *is on the other, nearest the
               saloon. They are shouting at each other across
               the intervening bodies.*)

ARTHUR   You'll bloody well do as you're told! I've had
               enough from you this evening.

MARY   Look out, Arthur!

SHIRLEY   It wasn't my fault. Ask her what happened, if you want to talk about it.

ARTHUR   (*losing his temper completely*) I won't tell you again - get inside before I drag you in by the hair, you little . . . !

           (*He is attempting to get hold of her, which causes further disruption just as* WENDY *and* CAROL *cross the gangplank.*)

MARY   Arthur!

JOHN   Look out!

CAROL   Careful!

           (*Suddenly there is a scream from* WENDY, *and she disappears off the gangplank. There is a loud splash, followed by a stunned silence.* JOHN *rushes to the side, and* CAROL *to the bank.*)

CAROL   Wendy! Are you all right?

JOHN   Wendy?

WENDY   (*off*) Glglgle!

JOHN   (*leaning over the bows*) You're all right. Grab my hand! I've got you. It's all right.

CAROL   (*kneeling on the bank*) Hold on, darling - you're quite safe. We'll get you up.

           (ARTHUR *turns furiously on* MARY.)

ARTHUR   This is all your fault!

           Blackout. End of Act One.

ACT TWO

Scene One

The next morning. Bright sunshine and river sounds. The bed in the saloon is made up, and the figures of SHIRLEY *and* WENDY *lie asleep under the covers.* CAROL *lies in bed in the guest cabin, awake, staring at the ceiling.* ARTHUR *sticks his head into the saloon from the passage. He cautiously crosses the saloon taking care not to wake the girls. He is dressed in casual clothes. He climbs up on deck, does a few token deep breaths and stretching exercises, and then sets off along the river bank at a brisk walk.*

There is the sound of a toilet flushing, and JOHN *comes out of the shower room, wearing pyjamas and dressing gown. He looks distinctly haggard. He looks at himself in the mirror, grimaces, and tries to do something with his tousled hair.*

CAROL	You look dreadful.
JOHN	Are you surprised? I didn't sleep a wink.
CAROL	Well you certainly stopped me from sleeping.
JOHN	I don't know how you *could* sleep, in the circumstances.
CAROL	There wasn't much we could do about it, was there?
JOHN	What do you mean?
CAROL	Well what could we do? Go after the boy and say, 'Please could we have our daughter's virginity back'?
JOHN	(*prim*) Carol, for God's sake . . .
CAROL	Well, what could we have done?
JOHN	We could have talked about it.
CAROL	We *did* talk - half the night.
JOHN	I mean, with Wendy.

CAROL	We *did* talk with Wendy.
JOHN	And with Shirley.
CAROL	What's the point of that? She was just an accessory.
JOHN	She was the ring-leader.
CAROL	Yes, well it sounds as if it's a fairly regular practice with her, so she wouldn't have been much use. Besides, she and Arthur were so busy shouting at each other, no one else could get a word in edgeways.
JOHN	God, what a family! How did we ever agree to this weekend? (*Sits on the bed.*) My head is splitting!
CAROL	(*stroking his head*) It's no wonder, darling. Tossing and turning and groaning all night. You'd think we'd all been sentenced to hang in the morning.
JOHN	Well, how do you expect me to react?
CAROL	It's not the end of the world, angel. She is seventeen.
JOHN	(*aghast*) She . . . !
CAROL	It had to go sometime.
JOHN	Good heavens, Carol - you talk as if she was getting rid of an old coat!
CAROL	It's the modern age.
JOHN	It doesn't have to happen like that. With some lout she hasn't even seen before! Besides - modern age or not, I thought we'd brought her up to live by our standards.
CAROL	What are our standards?

JOHN   What . . . ? Carol - do you have to ask me
            that?

CAROL   Well, I'm not sure I know really. I mean we
            pay reverential homage to some glowing,
            hypothetical ideal of morality - but I'm never
            quite sure what it actually *means*.

JOHN   It means . . . well, it means . . . it means not
            behaving like Wendy did last night! You'd
            never have behaved like that when you were
            her age.

CAROL   I did actually.

JOHN   What?

CAROL   I got had for the first time when I was
            seventeen.

JOHN   You told me you were a virgin when you met
            me.

CAROL   That was because you were so proper I
            thought you'd go off me if you knew I wasn't.

JOHN   Good lord! (*Pause.*) I . . .

CAROL   Yes?

JOHN   I honestly don't know what to say. (*She just
            smiles at him.*) Still, you would never have
            let yourself be taken by some oik you'd never
            met before - as Carol did.

CAROL   No. I'd known him for three days. He was an
            assistant decorator, who was doing up our
            lounge. (*Wistfully.*) He had black hair and
            lovely brown skin, I remember. I think he
            was part Greek, or something.

JOHN   (*dazed*) How . . . ? Why . . . ? How did it
            happen?

CAROL   What d'you mean, how?

JOHN   Well . . . where did you do it?

CAROL   On the dust sheets, on the lounge floor, in his
            lunch hour.

JOHN   Where was your mother?

CAROL   Out doing meals-on-wheels.

JOHN   You mean, he raped you while she was out?

CAROL   No, of course not - I was quite willing. In
            fact I enjoyed it enormously once I got the
            hang of it. We made it a regular thing while
            he was there. Every lunch time, while my
            mother was doing meals-on-wheels, and his
            mate was having his sandwiches in the van.
            (*Giggles.*) He made that decorating job last
            for weeks!

JOHN   (*faint*) Carol - I . . . I'm at a complete loss.

CAROL   (*patting him*) Well, I'm glad you know,
            darling. It's been very difficult living up to
            this saintly image of me you've always had.
            Now, I want some breakfast - I'm starving.

            (*She gets out of bed, and goes to the shower
            room. He remains sitting dazedly on the edge
            of the bed.* ARTHUR *returns along the bank
            carrying a newspaper. He boards the boat
            and cautiously enters the saloon. Sees that
            the girls are still asleep and no one else is
            present, and creeps into the galley to put the
            kettle on.* SHIRLEY *stirs in bed at the sounds,
            and makes waking-up noises.*)

ARTHUR   Shhh.

SHIRLEY   Oh, hello, Dad. What are you doing?

ARTHUR   What does it look like? I'm trying to make a
            cup of tea without waking up the boat.

SHIRLEY   Wassa time?

ARTHUR   (*looking apprehensively about him*) Shhhh!
                'Bout half past nine.

SHIRLEY   Well it's time they woke up then, isn't it?

ARTHUR   The later the better as far as I'm concerned.
                After what's happened I'm not particularly
                looking forward to meeting them.

SHIRLEY   (*blearily*) What *has* happened? (*He glares at
                her.*) Oh, that.

ARTHUR   (*in an angry whisper*) I know it's as trivial a
                business to you, by all accounts, as having a
                piece of toast for breakfast, young madam . . .

SHIRLEY   Oh don't start off again, Dad. We haven't
                even got up yet.

ARTHUR   But for most ordinary people - and that
                includes Wendy and her parents - it's not
                something to be dismissed with a shrug of the
                shoulders, like going out without an umbrella.

SHIRLEY   I don't use an umbrella.

ARTHUR   No, quite. And one of these days you're
                going to get very wet indeed.

SHIRLEY   Well you should know.

ARTHUR   What?

SHIRLEY   Risk getting pissed on yourself, sometimes,
                don't you?

ARTHUR   What is that supposed . . . ?

                (WENDY *stirs at the noise, and wakes up.*)

                Shhh.

WENDY   Oh, hello. Is it time to get up?

ARTHUR	No, no - you stay there as long as you want. You're on holiday - ha, ha.
WENDY	(*grimacing*) Oo - my head!
SHIRLEY	I'm not surprised.
WENDY	Why - what . . . ? (*Remembers.*) Oh, Lord . . .
ARTHUR	(*hastily*) I'll make you some coffee. That's what you need.
WENDY	What I need is the bathroom, I think. (*Starts to climb out of bed. She is wearing a long nightie.*) Oh. I haven't got a dressing gown.
SHIRLEY	Oh, for heaven's sake! You don't have to worry about things like that on a boat. (*She gets out of bed herself. She is wearing a short t-shirt and little else.*)
ARTHUR	Strikes me *you* ought to worry about things like that, my girl. That outfit doesn't leave much to the imagination.
SHIRLEY	All right, Dad. I'm changing into my bikini soon - will that make you feel better? Come on, Wendy. Bring your case - you can change in the bathroom. (*Goes off towards the passageway.*)
WENDY	(*uncertainly*) Oh . . . right. (*Follows with her case.*)
ARTHUR	(*as* SHIRLEY *opens the door*) Shhhh - don't wake her parents.
WENDY	Oh, I expect they're awake anyway. They never sleep late.
ARTHUR	(*uneasily*) Oh.

(*The girls go off.* ARTHUR *gets the tea ready,
with as much stealth as possible.* CAROL
*reappears from the shower room, and starts to
brush her hair in front of a mirror.*)

CAROL   I think I can hear noises. Do you suppose we
           can go and get some breakfast? I'm starving.

JOHN   I don't know how you can think of such
           things.

CAROL   Why?

           (*He says nothing.* MARY *appears in the
           saloon, dressed.*)

MARY   Oh, are the girls up?

ARTHUR   Shhhh! Do you want to wake up the whole
           boat?

MARY   Well, they're all awake anyway, aren't they?

ARTHUR   John and Carol aren't. At least they haven't
           shown themselves yet, and as far as I'm
           concerned, the later they do, the better.

MARY   Why?

ARTHUR   Why? Why d'you think? Everyone seems to
           have got amnesia this morning!

MARY   Well we've got to see them sometime. (*Going
           to the galley.*) Now how about some eggs and
           bacon? A good breakfast'll make all the
           difference.

ARTHUR   Oh yes, that's right. Come the nuclear
           holocaust all we have to do is cook a good
           breakfast for the troops.

MARY   Have you a better idea? (*Searching.*) I'll
           make some toast at least. Where's the bread?

ARTHUR   In the rope locker, I should think.

MARY   (*searching*) No - it's not there.

                (*He raises his eyes to the ceiling. She
                straightens up from the locker.*)

                By the way, Arthur, what were you doing up
                on deck with Carol at that time of night
                anyway?

ARTHUR   Eh? What d'you mean?

MARY   Well, you were up there when the girls came
                back, weren't you? It was a bit of a funny
                time.

ARTHUR   It was a nice night. We were just finishing
                our brandies and chatting, that's all.

MARY   Oh.

ARTHUR   Nothing wrong in that, is there? I was up
                there on my own, and she came out for a
                breath of air, that's all.

MARY   Ah. (*Finds the bread.*) Here it is - in the
                Calor gas cupboard. (*Puts some in the
                toaster.*)

ARTHUR   Bad luck on Wendy, mind. If her mother
                hadn't been there we might have been able to
                keep it all quiet.

MARY   Not with the amount of noise you made about
                it, you wouldn't. The whole river got the
                story.

ARTHUR   That was Shirley's fault. Always has to have
                the last word, that girl.

MARY   (*taking the bed clothes off the bunk*) Hmm.
                Give me a hand with this bunk, will you?
                We'd better get the table up for breakfast.

ARTHUR   (*obeying*) I mean, she couldn't even show
                any shame over it. I don't know what's the
                matter with the girl. No, Mary, that end goes
                in first - it's quite simple if you do it the right
                way.

                (*They pack the bunk away, and erect the
                table.*)

MARY   You just won't give her a chance, that's the
                trouble. You're so busy criticising her, you
                put her on the defensive all the time.

ARTHUR   What am I supposed to do after something
                like that? Say well done, girl - splendid
                effort - carry on the good work? She's got
                the teenage daughter of our guests had rotten
                with a possible bun in the oven, and from all
                accounts she's added to a pretty impressive
                list of conquests on her own account as well -
                am I supposed to give her an award for long-
                standing service to her country? Eh?

MARY   Of course not.

ARTHUR   Well then . . . See that end's in properly, or
                we'll have the whole ruddy lot on the floor. I
                mean, how long has this sort of thing been
                going on?

MARY   She is seventeen, Arthur.

ARTHUR   What's that supposed to mean?

MARY   She's a woman. (*Begins to load breakfast
                things onto a tray.*)

ARTHUR   She's a child! She's a baby! What age do
                they start nowadays - as soon as they're out of
                rompers?

MARY   You had me when I was seventeen.

ARTHUR   I nev . . . Did I?

MARY   Yes. Seventeen. Caused a dreadful row with
                my parents, if you remember. Especially as
                you were engaged to Sally Moffat at the time.

ARTHUR   (*abashed*) Well, that's different. We were in
                love.

MARY   No, we weren't. You were engaged to
                somebody else, and I was drunk. You just
                took advantage of me. Not much different to
                last night, if you ask me.

ARTHUR   At least I knew who you were. We were
                dating regularly, and . . .

MARY   It was our second time out. You got me drunk
                on Babycham, and had my knickers off on
                your mac in Epping Forest . . .

ARTHUR   (*looking fearfully towards the cabins*) Shhhh!

MARY   . . . so you can't claim to be any better than
                anyone else.

ARTHUR   (*furious*) Look, whose side are you on over
                this? Are you saying you *approve* of last
                night?

MARY   I'm just saying we've no right to get all moral
                and self-righteous over it. I agree it shouldn't
                have happened, but it did. These things do.
                That's all. (*Brings the tray to the table.*)

ARTHUR   For Christ's sake, Mary . . .

                (*As MARY puts the tray on the table, the latter
                collapses and deposits the breakfast things on
                the floor with a deafening crash. Deathly
                silence.*)

                Bloody hell, woman - I *told* you to fix the end
                in properly!

                (*JOHN and CAROL have heard the crash, and
                leave their cabin to investigate.*)

MARY   (*calmly*) That's your end that gave way, Arthur, not mine.

ARTHUR   It was nothing of the . . . (*Sees she is right.*) Well if it was, it was you distracting me that did it. I can't believe my ears this morning. Morality's gone out of the window! The whole world's turned upside down! I don't . . .

                (MARY *notices* JOHN *and* CAROL'S *heads peering round the corner from the passageway.*)

MARY   Good morning.

ARTHUR   (*turning*) Ah, good morning. Come and join the party. We always throw crockery around the place on a Sunday morning - helps wake us all up.

                (*They enter hesitantly.* MARY *starts to pick up the mess.*)

CAROL   Let me help you. (*Goes to help.*)

MARY   Thank you.

ARTHUR   Cup of tea on the side there, John. At least that survived the crash. Help yourself.

JOHN   Thank you. (*Pours himself some tea.*)

ARTHUR   Sleep well?

JOHN   Not very.

ARTHUR   Oh dear. Bunk not comfortable?

JOHN   I just had other things on my mind.

ARTHUR   Ah yes - well . . . (*To* MARY.) Not too much broken, is there?

MARY   Only the marmalade.

ARTHUR   Oh my God! Make sure you get it all off the
                carpet. It cost a fortune.

CAROL   The marmalade?

ARTHUR   The carpet, you . . . (*Controls himself.*)

CAROL   Oh.

                (JOHN *comes down stage with his tea.* ARTHUR
                follows.)

ARTHUR   I'm sorry, John . . . about everything. This
                weekend hasn't turned out quite as we, er . . .

JOHN   No, well . . . things don't always - do they?

ARTHUR   To be frank, I don't know what to do about
                our Shirley. I sometimes think things were
                easier in the old days. Boy or girl, you'd
                have given them a jolly good hiding, and
                everyone would have forgotten about it and
                sat down to the Sunday joint with no more
                ado.

JOHN   I don't think that's quite the solution
                somehow.

ARTHUR   No, no, of course not, but er . . . Well,
                anyway I'm sorry. Really nice girl, Wendy.
                Didn't deserve such, er . . .

CAROL   It takes two.

                (JOHN *glares at her.*)

ARTHUR   Well, yes of course, but er . . . Well, Wendy's
                not that type.

CAROL   What type?

ARTHUR   Well - to, er . . .

CAROL   Are you suggesting she was raped?

ARTHUR   No, of course not, but . . .

CAROL   Well then.

JOHN   (*warningly*) Carol.

MARY   Anyway - Shirley's not that type either.

                (*No one can think of anything to say to that.*)

                Now who'd like some breakfast? Eggs and
                bacon, John? Carol?

JOHN   No, thank you. Just some tea and a piece of
                toast will do fine.

ARTHUR   Come on - you're on holiday. Why not
                indulge a bit?

JOHN   I don't honestly think we feel like more
                indulging, thank you.

CAROL   Oh, what the hell - I'll have eggs and bacon -
                why not?

                (JOHN *glares again. She looks defiant.*)

MARY   Oh good. (*Goes to the galley area.*) Arthur?

ARTHUR   Yes, I'll keep Carol company. We're only
                young once. (*Mutters at her.*) And try not to
                fry the bacon to a frazzle. (*Turns to the
                others.*) Now sit down, folks. Have some
                orange juice while you're waiting.

CAROL   (*sitting*) Thank you.

MARY   (*fiddling with the matches*) Arthur - I can't
                get the gas to light.

ARTHUR   (*to the others, with a sigh*) I don't know.
                Why is it . . . ? Here - give it to me. (*Tries
                to light it himself.*) What the . . . ? Oh, no.
                The bloody gas has run out.

MARY   (*dismayed*) Oh, Arthur.

ARTHUR   It's all right - there's a spare . . . (*Stops.*)

MARY   No, there isn't. That *was* the spare. We
                didn't bring another one.

                (ARTHUR *looks frantically in the gas cylinder
                cupboard.*)

ARTHUR   (*his temper rising*) I don't believe it! It's not
                possible! It's Sunday morning - miles from
                anywhere - and you're telling me there's no
                gas to cook with? What about breakfast?
                Never mind breakfast - what about lunch?
                What about the roast lamb and new potatoes?

MARY   I told you we should have had salad. But no,
                you insisted. Proper Sunday lunch you
                wanted.

ARTHUR   Well naturally. It's Sunday.

MARY   Well, we'll just have to think of another way.

ARTHUR   How? Chop up some of the boat and light a
                bonfire? Know how to do roast lamb and all
                the trimmings on a burning boat, do you?
                This is beyond belief! How can we have run
                out?

MARY   Well, we cooked a big dinner last night. And
                everyone's been having showers after all that
                swimming around in the river afterwards.

ARTHUR   Why didn't you remember to bring another
                cylinder?

MARY   That's your job.

ARTHUR   I can't think of everything. Why didn't you
                remind me? (*Turns to the others.*) I'm very
                sorry, folks. It's normally automatic to have
                a spare one in.

CAROL   We'll just have to go out for lunch. What
            about that pub?

JOHN   I'm not sure a return to that pub is a very
            good idea.

CAROL   Well there must be somewhere else.

ARTHUR   No, no, I refuse. You're supposed to be our
            guests, on our boat. There must be
            somewhere we can find a spare cylinder.
            Every boat on the river uses them, for God's
            sake!

MARY   Well, you'd better go up the river bank and
            ask if any of them will let you have one.

            (SHIRLEY *and* WENDY *return from the
            bathroom.* SHIRLEY *is wearing a very brief
            bikini, and carries a light beach jacket.*
            WENDY *is dressed in shorts and summer top -
            more modest, but only just.*)

SHIRLEY   Dad, there's no hot water in the bathroom.

ARTHUR   I know there's no hot water in the bathroom!
            There's no hot water anywhere!

SHIRLEY   Why not?

ARTHUR   Because you lot have used it all, that's why,
            and . . .

MARY   And because your father forgot to bring a
            spare Calor gas cylinder.

SHIRLEY   Ah.

ARTHUR   (*rounding on her*) And that's hardly a decent
            outfit for breakfast, young woman.

SHIRLEY   We don't want any breakfast. We're just
            going up on deck.

ARTHUR   On deck?

SHIRLEY	It's a lovely day. We're going to sunbathe.
ARTHUR	(*looking at his watch*) What? At . . .
CAROL	(*interrupting*) What a good idea! I might join you later.
ARTHUR	Oh.
SHIRLEY	(*to* WENDY) Come on. (*Heads for the door to the deck.*)
ARTHUR	Hold on - I've got a job for you first.
SHIRLEY	What's that?
ARTHUR	I want you to ask along the other boats if anyone will sell us a gas cylinder. We can't cook lunch until we find one.
SHIRLEY	Sure you trust us out on our own, Dad?
ARTHUR	No, I don't, but I'm hoping you've learnt your lesson.
SHIRLEY	Right. (*Turns again.*)
ARTHUR	Not like that though. Go and put some clothes on first.
SHIRLEY	Why? What's wrong as we are?
ARTHUR	You're touting for Calor gas, not body beautiful awards.
SHIRLEY	Don't be so prudish, Dad.
ARTHUR	Look, after what happened last night . . .
MARY	Oh, don't fuss, Arthur.
ARTHUR	(*surprised*) What? Now look . . . (*Turns to* JOHN *for support.*) John?
JOHN	I must say . . .

CAROL (*interrupting*) Oh, let them go. They'll probably have more chance of getting some gas like that.

ARTHUR They'll have more chance of getting all sorts of things like that! I . . .

SHIRLEY (*slipping on her beach jacket*) Oh come on, Wendy - it'll be lunch time already by the time they've finished arguing.

(*Grabs* WENDY'S *hand, and leads her up on deck before* ARTHUR *can protest any more.*)

ARTHUR I give up. I just give up with this family.

MARY Yes, it's probably about time you did. (*Puts toast on the table.*) Now then - John, Carol - have some more tea, and help yourself to toast. We have still got electricity at least.

ARTHUR Fine - let's slice up the lamb and cook it in the toaster.

(*All except* ARTHUR *sit round the table, and start on the toast.*)

MARY Marmalade, Carol?

CAROL Thank you.

MARY More tea, John?

JOHN Thank you.

ARTHUR (*unable to contain his impatience*) Bring your tea up on deck, John. It's too nice a day to sit down here.

JOHN (*uncertainly*) Oh.

ARTHUR We can keep an eye on those girls at the same time. Here, I'll bring your toast.

                    (*Grabs* JOHN's *plate, giving him no option but
                    to follow.*)

JOHN   Oh, well . . . (*To the women.*) Excuse us.

                    (*They go up onto the fore-deck.*)

MARY   (*apologetically to* CAROL) I expect he wants
                    to talk business. Never did know the meaning
                    of patience.

CAROL   Ah.

MARY   More tea?

CAROL   No, thank you - I'm fine.

ARTHUR   (*up on deck, peering off along the river bank*)
                    Now where the devil have they got to? Can't
                    see them, can you?

JOHN   They must be on board one of the boats.

ARTHUR   Well, that'll liven up somebody's Sunday
                    morning, eh?

JOHN   Yes.

CAROL   (*down below*) I think I'll go and put some
                    clothes on.

MARY   Oh. Had enough breakfast?

CAROL   Yes, thank you. That was lovely.

                    (*She goes off to the cabin, collects some
                    clothes, and takes them into the shower room.*
                    MARY *starts clearing the breakfast things.*)

ARTHUR   I'm very sorry about everything, John.

JOHN   Look, you've already apologised. There's
                    honestly nothing much we can do about it, is
                    there? Let's leave it at that.

ARTHUR   Yes, but all the same . . . ah, well. There's
              your toast. (*Hands it to him.*)

JOHN   Thank you.

              (ARTHUR *turns and takes a deep breath.*)

ARTHUR   Ah - that's better. Lovely morning.

JOHN   Yes.

ARTHUR   I love the river at this time. Smells so fresh.

JOHN   Yes.

ARTHUR   Thought any more about my little project,
              have you, John?

JOHN   Not really. What with one thing and another . . .

ARTHUR   Yes, quite - but, er . . . well I'd like you to
              give it some serious thought, you know.

JOHN   (*non-committally*) Mm.

ARTHUR   You see, you probably don't quite understand
              just how important that scheme is to me,
              John.

JOHN   Oh?

ARTHUR   I've been nursing Garrett's along for years -
              doing various small developments for them.
              But this is the really big one. If I can pull
              this one off, it'll set me up for the rest of my
              life.

JOHN   Really?

ARTHUR   If I miss it I doubt if I'll get another chance.

JOHN   Surely there'll be other opportunities.

ARTHUR   Well, you see . . . I've had enough, quite
              frankly, John.

JOHN   Enough?

ARTHUR   I wouldn't say this to many people, but
                mine's a bloody awful business to be in.

JOHN   You seem to have done all right from it.

ARTHUR   Oh, I've made a reasonable living over the
                years. But it's not exactly . . . it's not . . .
                what I'd call fulfilling.

JOHN   Fulfilling?

ARTHUR   I sometimes see myself looking back in old
                age, and saying to myself - 'What have you
                created in your life that the world will
                remember, Arthur Bullhead?' And back will
                come the answer, 'Three launderettes, a
                couple of office blocks, and a plastic bag
                factory.'

JOHN   What would you do instead?

ARTHUR   (*holding his arms out to the river*) I'd enjoy
                life. I'd do all the things I've been saying I'd
                do for years, and never got around to. Of
                course I'd probably carry on with the odd
                development, but only the sort that matters to
                me.

JOHN   What sort is that?

ARTHUR   Refurbishing old buildings. That's what I'm
                really good at. I can take a derelict
                farmhouse, or a forgotten Georgian terrace,
                and transform it back two hundred years. I
                tell you, John, there's no thrill like seeing
                some clapped out old ruin come to life again,
                and glow with history and character like it
                used to.

JOHN   Like this boat, you mean?

ARTHUR   Well, after a fashion. I had fun renovating this. The decor's Mary's, and, bless her, she hasn't quite got the touch. But I let her have her head because it kept her busy.

JOHN   I see.

ARTHUR   Of course you could change all that.

JOHN   Change it?

ARTHUR   When the boat became yours.

JOHN   Oh, I don't think . . .

ARTHUR   I'm serious, John, I want this scheme to go through. I'll put my cards on the table. It's worth half a million pounds to me. Enough to see us comfortable for the rest of our lives. And if you can make that happen, then it's only fair that you should have a share in the benefits. I want you to think seriously about my proposition.

JOHN   I have thought seriously about it.

ARTHUR   And?

JOHN   To be quite honest, I think it's the most unethical suggestion I've ever heard.

ARTHUR   Oh, now John . . .

JOHN   I've wondered whether there was any legal way I could take action over it, but unfortunately - as I don't suppose you'd be stupid enough to put it into writing - I don't think there is.

ARTHUR   Action?

JOHN   However the one thing I can do is to see that you have as small a chance of winning the scheme as possible. Strangely - although, as

chairman of the various committees you
mentioned, I have less ability to push
proposals through than you imagine - I do
have considerably more influence when it
comes to getting them rejected. Such are the
ways of local politics. It's always easier to
hinder things than help them.

ARTHUR   But why? Why would you do that?

JOHN   Because you're an immoral man. And
            immorality must be fought in this world -
            wherever and whenever it occurs.

ARTHUR   Immoral?

JOHN   Yes.

ARTHUR   Just because I offer you a reward? Because I
            offer to make you a partner in something
            that's going to benefit the whole community?

JOHN   That's debatable. In any case, it's not just
            that. It's your whole attitude to life. It's
            your opportunistic, get-rich-quick, if-you-
            can't-beat-'em-buy-'em-out mentality. It
            epitomises what's wrong with the modern
            world.

ARTHUR   (totally at a loss) I don't understand, I don't
            follow. How can what I do be immoral?
            Because I don't get paid a regular salary?
            Because I'm not a member of some Royal
            Society Of Property Speculators? If it wasn't
            for people like me, people like you wouldn't
            have any work yourselves.

JOHN   What do you mean?

ARTHUR   It's us that gets all your High Street
            developments, and your dockland ventures,
            and your new housing projects off the ground.
            You only do the bloody paperwork. We're
            the ones who have the imagination to see the
            chances, and the guts to take the risk. Tell

me this - what'll happen if Garrett's don't get
their store there. You'll get Jack Craddock in
instead, with one of his great concrete and
glass monstrosities . . .

JOHN   Not necessarily. I don't honestly think we
              want either of them.

ARTHUR   What? Is there someone else in the running?

JOHN   No. I'm just saying I'm not persuaded the
              town needs a supermarket anyway. They're
              just another soulless, modern, so-called
              convenience foisted upon people by
              entrepreneurs such as yourself, who don't
              really give a damn for the good of the
              community. What about all the small
              shopkeepers who've served that community
              for generations, and who'll be put out of
              business by the project?

ARTHUR   They'll go out of business anyway if they
              don't move with the times.

JOHN   The times? What do you mean, move with
              the times?

ARTHUR   Well . . .

JOHN   Who *wants* to move with the times? They're
              bloody awful times. I hate the wretched
              times!

              (*Pause.*)

ARTHUR   Ah.

JOHN   Don't you?

ARTHUR   No. I quite like the times actually.

JOHN   Huh! Yes, I suppose you would.

ARTHUR   Damn sight better than my old man's times
              anyway. And his old man's before him, too.

JOHN   Yes, well . . . that's as maybe. But at least
            they had ethics then. They had a code of
            morality.

ARTHUR   Bollocks! My old man was a butcher. And
            during the war rationing he ran the smartest
            little black market operation you've ever
            seen. It was the only way he managed to keep
            us above the poverty line.

JOHN   Yes - well that's not surprising. Like father,
            like son.

ARTHUR   You what?

JOHN   And like father, like daughter too.

ARTHUR   Now look here . . .

JOHN   No, I won't support your application. Or Jack
            Craddock's. He's as bad as you are. We
            don't want people like you in our town.

ARTHUR   (*after a moment*) You hypocrite.

JOHN   What?

ARTHUR   You toffee-nosed, hypocritical bag of
            bullshit! Rabbiting on about morals and
            ethics and all the rest . . . When you're just as
            bad as the rest of us.

JOHN   I beg your pardon.

ARTHUR   Tell me, does Craddock know how you
            diddled him, eh?

JOHN   What do you mean?

ARTHUR   I'm talking about his petrol station deal.
            Does he know how you used his cash to save
            your own scrawny neck? Does he know how
            much you cost him in order to get yourself out

of your own incompetent mess all those years ago? Well?

(JOHN *has gone white, and leans against the boat's roof for support.*)

Yeh, that shook you, didn't it?

JOHN	What are you talking about?
ARTHUR	You know.
JOHN	How did you know about . . . ?
ARTHUR	I make it my business to know about people. Finish your toast.

(JOHN *almost chokes at the thought.* ARTHUR *takes it instead.*)

Well, now that all the cards are on the table . . . Now that we don't need to have any more pretence about scruples, and morality, and so forth - let's talk plainly, shall we? Or should I say 'honestly'? It looks like you've got a simple choice. My scheme for Garrett's, or Jack Craddock's for Thames Stores.

JOHN   (*almost a whisper*) What do you mean?

ARTHUR   Either I get my scheme through - and settle down to a happy semi-retirement - while you enjoy some leisure time on your nice boat - or else I tell Jack Craddock what I know about your client's account with his money in it. In which case I'm quite sure that, being far more unscrupulous than I am, he'll use the information to persuade you to see that *his* scheme gets through. (*Pauses to let it sink in.*) Seems to me you're caught between the Devil and the deep blue sea. (*Grins.*) Or in this case the developer and the dirty grey Thames.

JOHN   You're blackmailing me.

ARTHUR   (*cheerfully*) Yes. Honestly.

                (*Pause.* JOHN *sits, weakly.* ARTHUR *looks
                about him.*)

                Whew! Going to be a scorcher today. I think
                the girls are right - it's shirts off, and a spot
                of suntan this morning. What do you say?

                (*No answer.* ARTHUR *looks along the bank.*)

                Ah - talking of devils - here they come.
                Successful too, by the look of it.

                (*The girls appear, carrying a Calor gas
                cylinder between them. They totter across the
                gangplank with it.*)

                Careful now. Take it steady.

SHIRLEY   Pfff! I hope this is worth it. You'd never
                believe what we had to go through to get this.

ARTHUR   Where'd it come from?

SHIRLEY   A dirty old man living on that ancient rotting
                houseboat up there. We practically had to
                sell our bodies to get it, didn't we, Wend?

WENDY   (*giggling*) Yes.

ARTHUR   I'm not surprised - dressed like that. I
                warned you.

SHIRLEY   Yes, Dad. Well it did the trick anyway. And
                he doesn't even want paying for it.

ARTHUR   He doesn't?

SHIRLEY   Just said to be sure to bring the empty
                cylinder back. (*With a glance at* WENDY.)
                And he might even give us something for it.
                (*They giggle.*)

ARTHUR   (*picking up the cylinder*) Well I'll take it
              down, so your mother can get on with the
              lunch.

WENDY   (*looking at* JOHN's *depressed figure*) Are you
              all right, Daddy?

ARTHUR   He's feeling a bit seasick, that's all.

              (*Takes the cylinder below.*)

WENDY   Seasick?

JOHN   (*pulling himself together*) I'm all right.

SHIRLEY   Shall I get you a cup of coffee, or some . . .

JOHN   (*irritably*) I'm perfectly all right, thank you!

SHIRLEY   (*taken aback*) All right. (*Awkward pause.*)
              Well, I think it's time for a bit of sunbathing,
              don't you, Wendy? Let's go on top.

              (*She starts to climb the ladder to the roof.*
              WENDY *goes to follow.*)

JOHN   (*to* WENDY) Just keep yourself decent, will
              you? There are other people within sight.

SHIRLEY   (*deliberately provocative*) Oh, that's all
              right. People even go topless on the river
              these days.

              (JOHN *can think of nothing to say to that, and
              goes below, looking black as thunder.*
              SHIRLEY *and* WENDY *giggle conspiratorially to
              each other, light up cigarettes, and settle
              down on the sun mattresses to sunbathe.* JOHN
              storms through the saloon towards his cabin.
              MARY *turns from the sink to watch him, and*
              ARTHUR *straightens up from the gas cylinder
              cupboard. They look at each other as* JOHN
              goes out to the corridor.)

MARY	What's the matter with him?
ARTHUR	Oh dear. I hope . . . (*Breaks off.*)
MARY	What? What have you done now, Arthur?
ARTHUR	Shhh!

(Goes to the saloon bulkhead, and puts his ear to the wall. MARY follows, and listens curiously. JOHN bursts into the cabin, and marches across to the shower room door. He pounds on it with his fist.)

| JOHN | Carol! Come out of there! |

(CAROL comes out, dressed, and carrying a hairbrush.)

CAROL	What's the matter?
JOHN	You told him!
CAROL	What?
JOHN	You told Bullhead about my client's account crisis. It must have been you. No one else knows.
CAROL	(*caught off balance*) I . . .
JOHN	Why? How could you do such a thing?
CAROL	I . . . I didn't mean to, John. It was just . . .
JOHN	Bullhead! Of all people! How could you?
CAROL	We were just chatting. He's a nice man really . . .
JOHN	He's a monster!
CAROL	No, John - he's quite nice underneath. He was upset that his family wasn't as happy as ours on the surface, and I was trying to reassure him that we have our problems too, and . . .

JOHN   You discuss our private affairs with that lump
            of dog turd!

CAROL   (*shocked*) John!

ARTHUR   (*next door, muttering*) Thanks a lot!

JOHN   That . . . that . . . low-bred, smart-alec,
            cheap-jack, spiv!

ARTHUR   Here - steady on.

CAROL   He's nothing of the kind! He's . . .

JOHN   He's a blackmailer! That's what he is.

CAROL   Blackmailer?

JOHN   He's using that information to force me to
            support his scheme. And you gave it to him!

CAROL   Oh, John!

JOHN   You bitch!

            (*He slaps her face. There is a moment's
            stunned silence. Then she slaps him back. He
            is equally stunned. Raises his hand to hit her
            again. She does likewise. A moment's
            impasse. Then she pushes him out of the way,
            and marches out of the cabin. He sits on the
            bed, bemused. She enters the saloon.* ARTHUR
            goes towards her apologetically.)

ARTHUR   Carol, I . . .

            (*Without breaking her stride she clouts him as
            well, and continues on across the saloon, and
            up on deck.* ARTHUR *staggers back, his hand
            to his nose.*)

            Oh God - it's bleeding!

            (*Fishes for a handkerchief.* MARY *goes to
            help. Waves her away.*)

Get on with the lunch - I'll handle it.

(*Goes towards the cabins. Turns in the doorway, and talks through his handkerchief.*)

And for heaven's sake don't overcook the lamb this time!

(*Goes off.* MARY *starts to lay the table for lunch. Up on the fore-deck* CAROL *is standing, staring angrily out across the river. The two girls look up from their sun mattresses, and hurriedly put out their cigarettes.*)

WENDY   Mummy? Are you all right?

CAROL   (*turning*) Oh. I didn't see you there.

WENDY   What's happened?

CAROL   I've just had a little tiff with Daddy, that's all.

WENDY   A tiff? What about?

CAROL   Nothing important.

WENDY   But you never have rows.

CAROL   It wasn't really a row, darling . . .

WENDY   What was it then?

CAROL   It was . . . a row.

WENDY   Was it to do with the row he was having with Mr Bullhead?

CAROL   Was he?

WENDY   It looked like it. Didn't it, Shirley?

SHIRLEY   Yes. But then everyone has rows with Dad.

CAROL   It could have been.

WENDY	What was it about?
CAROL	I'd rather not talk about it just now. Have you two been smoking up there?
WENDY	Er . . . well . . .
CAROL	Really going to town this weekend, aren't you? (*Turns back to the river.*)

(SHIRLEY *nudges* WENDY.)

WENDY	Mum?
CAROL	Yes?
WENDY	Can I ask you something?
CAROL	What?
WENDY	Please don't get cross.
CAROL	(*turning*) What is it?
WENDY	(*hesitantly*) Well . . . you know those two boys Shirley and I . . . saw last night.
CAROL	Yes.
WENDY	Well, we sort of bumped into them again just now . . . along the river.
CAROL	(*peering up-river*) Bumped into?
WENDY	Well, they were waiting for us.
CAROL	And?
WENDY	They're not at all what you all think they are, Mummy. I know they dress a bit funny, and they've got modern hairstyles . . .
CAROL	Modern? Looked quite historic to me. Inca period possibly.

WENDY   But they really are very nice when you get to know them. One's a boat-builder. Knows all about racing yachts, and plans to sail round the world single-handed one day. And the other . . . mine . . . Roger he's called . . .

CAROL   Very suitable. (*Repentant.*) Sorry.

WENDY   He works with horses.

CAROL   Horses?

WENDY   Yes. On a stud farm.

CAROL   (*after a moment*) I haven't said a thing. You mean he's a stable boy.

WENDY   Well, more than that, I think. He actually helps breed them. You wouldn't believe how much he knows about horses. He wants to have his own stud one day.

(CAROL *bites her lips shut.*)

CAROL   Well, what about them?

WENDY   They . . . (*Breaks off, and looks at* SHIRLEY.)

SHIRLEY   They want to see us again.

CAROL   When?

SHIRLEY   This morning.

WENDY   Just for a drink. At the pub.

CAROL   And you want to see them?

WENDY   Of course we do. We wouldn't have . . . unless we liked them.

CAROL   I suppose not.

WENDY   They're ever so nice, Mummy. I couldn't say so last night, but Roger was terribly sweet and thoughtful to me . . .

CAROL   (*distant*) Of course.

WENDY   He really liked me, I think. He wasn't just after a quick . . . you know. In fact he was almost as inexperienced as I was. We just got . . . carried away.

CAROL   Yes.

WENDY   I wasn't able to talk about it last night - there was so much shouting going on . . .

SHIRLEY   It's our normal method of communication, I'm afraid.

WENDY   Oh, don't worry, I wish I could have done some shouting myself. (*To* CAROL.) I would have liked to say . . . well, to tell you both that it was all right. That actually - although I know we shouldn't have done it . . . it was all right. But I couldn't.

(CAROL *just stands, looking away, a hint of tears in her eyes.* WENDY *pauses for a moment, then continues.*)

Well, I just wondered if there was any chance . . . I mean it doesn't seem right not to see them again. Especially when they came along specially to try and find us. I mean, surely it would have been worse if they'd just . . . forgotten all about it. (*Pause.*) Wouldn't it?

CAROL   (*quietly*) Yes.

WENDY   So . . . could we go, do you think? Just for a drink - I promise.

CAROL   (*turning back to her*) Yes, darling. You go.

WENDY   (*gratefully*) Oh, Mummy . . . !

CAROL   I can't answer for your parents of course, Shirley. Though I suspect you're father won't

	be in the mood to start moralising this morning.
SHIRLEY	That's all right. I'll find a way.
WENDY	What about Daddy?
CAROL	(*looking at her watch*) Well, it's after ten now. Do you know where the boys will be?
WENDY	Just along the river somewhere, I think. They were going to do some fishing till the pub opened.
CAROL	Well if you go now, your fathers won't find out until too late, will they?
WENDY	(*jumping up*) Oh, thank you, Mummy. (*Climbs down the ladder.*)
CAROL	Mind you're back for lunch. Although I can't promise quite where we'll be having it.
SHIRLEY	Aren't you having it with us?
CAROL	That depends on how things develop from now on, I'm afraid.
SHIRLEY	Oh. (*Follows* WENDY *down the ladder.*)
WENDY	(*on the deck*) The pub won't be open yet.
CAROL	Then you'll have to find something to do till it is - won't you? (*Smiles.*) Just see that - whatever you do - you don't . . . go overboard. After all, if you go out to sea it's up to you to be responsible about safety and so forth, isn't it?
WENDY	Yes, Mummy. (*Kisses her.*) Thank you.
SHIRLEY	Tell my dad we've gone to take some fishing lessons.

(*They go off along the river. CAROL watches them for a moment. Then she turns and goes below. MARY turns from the cooker as she enters the saloon.*)

MARY   Oh, I'm glad you're still here. I thought you might have abandoned ship.

CAROL   I'm sorry about Arthur. Did I hurt him?

MARY   (*happily*) Yes, I think you did quite. Serves him right.

CAROL   Well . . .

MARY   I wish I'd had the courage to do that a few times.

CAROL   I've never done it before. I hit John too.

MARY   Oh, well done!

CAROL   Mind you, he hit me first.

MARY   And I thought you were such a happy family.

CAROL   We were. At least I think we were.

MARY   Where are the girls?

CAROL   Gone fishing.

MARY   Fishing?

CAROL   Yes. They, er . . . met some old acquaintances of theirs, who offered to show them a bit more of life on the river.

MARY   (*after a moment*) I see.

CAROL   It obviously meant quite a lot to them. Both parties. I said they could go - as long as they didn't get in too deep.

MARY   Ah.

CAROL	I hope that was all right.
MARY	Why not?
	(*They smile at each other.* ARTHUR *appears from the corridor, still dabbing at his nose.*)
	Has it stopped bleeding?
ARTHUR	More or less.
CAROL	Oh, Arthur - I'm sorry.
ARTHUR	It's all right. I deserved it. I'm sorry, I didn't mean to spill the beans. I'm afraid I lost my temper when your old man started moralising.
CAROL	Ah, yes, I know the feeling.
	(*Next door,* JOHN *gets up and leaves the cabin.*)
ARTHUR	Well - how about a drink?
MARY	It's a bit early, Arthur.
ARTHUR	I don't care. I think we all need one.
CAROL	Good idea.
	(*As* ARTHUR *goes to the drinks,* JOHN *appears.*)
JOHN	Oh. You're all here.
ARTHUR	Yep. We've decided it's half-time. We're having a drink.
JOHN	Are the girls still up top?
ARTHUR	Yes.
CAROL	No.
JOHN	What?
CAROL	They've gone off for the morning.

ARTHUR	Gone off?
JOHN	Where?
CAROL	With their boyfriends.
JOHN	I beg your pardon?
CAROL	I said it was all right. (*They all stare at her. She shrugs.*) Well . . . I thought they may as well be hung for a sheep as for a lamb.

(*The bottle in* ARTHUR'S *hand falls with a crash onto the drinks tray. Blackout.*)

Scene Two

Later that morning. Both families are seated round the dining table, lunch almost finished. (NB: MARY *can have laid the table for lunch in the previous scene, so only a minimal amount of setting needs to be done in the scene change.) The silence is painful.* ARTHUR *clears his throat and signals at* MARY.

MARY	Well now - who's for more gateau? John?
JOHN	No, thank you.
CAROL	Not for me, thank you.
MARY	Wendy?
WENDY	No, thank you.
MARY	Shirley?

(SHIRLEY *just looks.* MARY *shrugs, and takes the plates to the sink.*)

I'll make some coffee then.

| ARTHUR | (*attempting to lift the proceedings*) Very nice lunch, Mary love. The lamb was done to a turn. |

CAROL	Yes - delicious.
ARTHUR	So, Wendy, he's a jockey, is he - this feller of yours?
MARY	(*warningly*) Arthur.
WENDY	A breeder.
ARTHUR	A breeder?
WENDY	Yes.
ARTHUR	You mean he's actually responsible for . . . ?
WENDY	Well, he works for a very rich businessman who owns a stud. Arab horses. On the other side of the river.
ARTHUR	Ah. And what does he actually do?
MARY	Arthur!
ARTHUR	(*wickedly*) No, I'm interested, Mary. I've always liked horses. (*To* CAROL.) Wouldn't be caught dead on top of one, mind you, but they're beautiful animals. (*She doesn't answer. He turns back to* WENDY.) So what does he do at this stud farm?
WENDY	Well, he calls himself a breeder, but I think really he's sort of head groom.
ARTHUR	Ah.
WENDY	But he plans to have his own stud one day. He's just mad about horses.
ARTHUR	Well, he sounds an intelligent fellow. Eh, Carol?
CAROL	Yes.

(JOHN *rises suddenly from his chair, looking black. He picks up one of* ARTHUR'S *boat magazines, and sits in an armchair, flicking angrily through the pages.*)

ARTHUR   Good magazine that, John. There's an article about converted barges which might interest you.

(JOHN *throws the magazine down.* ARTHUR *turns innocently back to* SHIRLEY.)

And yours is a boat man himself, is he, Shirl?

SHIRLEY   Yes.

ARTHUR   I must, er . . . What's his name?

SHIRLEY   Darren.

ARTHUR   I must meet Darren sometime. There's quite a bit I'd like to ask him about boats.

SHIRLEY   Why not? He'll probably be around a bit in future, so you can.

ARTHUR   Oh good. Knows all about the latest techniques, I expect, eh?. Shaping of the body work . . . mast heights . . . docking methods . . .

JOHN   Oh for God's sake!

ARTHUR   (*innocently*) I'm sorry, John - did I say something?

JOHN   I honestly think this has gone beyond a joke!

ARTHUR   What, John?

JOHN   This whole charade. This . . . this . . . debacle of a weekend. (*Rises.*) It's time we left.

ARTHUR   Debacle? Well, I'm sorry you feel that way
          about our hospitality. I know we've had the
          odd set-back, but Mary's put a lot of work
          into this weekend . . .

JOHN   I've nothing against Mary. Thank you for all
          your efforts, Mary. But I think, in all
          honesty, we should stop beating about the
          bush, and call it a day now.

ARTHUR   You feel that?

JOHN   Yes, I do.

ARTHUR   Carol? Do you feel that?

CAROL   Well . . .

ARTHUR   In all honesty? To be quite honest? I
          mean . . . honestly?

CAROL   No. I've quite enjoyed myself actually.

ARTHUR   Oh, well that's a relief.

CAROL   I've enjoyed myself rather a lot in fact.

ARTHUR   Wendy? Have you in all honesty enjoyed
          yourself?

WENDY   Yes. Honestly.

          (SHIRLEY *sniggers*.)

ARTHUR   Well, two out of three. Not too bad, eh John?

JOHN   (*to* CAROL) I don't know how you can do it.

CAROL   What?

JOHN   Pander to this man. Play his outrageous
          games.

ARTHUR   Games? I'm not playing games. This is life,
          John. The real thing.

JOHN   It may be life to you, but it's not our sort of life, I can assure you.

ARTHUR   Oh. And what is your sort of life? No, really, I'm interested.

JOHN   You wouldn't understand if I told you.

ARTHUR   Well I might. But so far I haven't had the chance. I mean, to be quite honest myself, John, I'm at a loss to know what it is you want from life. I've learnt a lot this weekend about what you *don't* want - about all the things you disapprove of - but not very much about what you're for.

JOHN   I'm for a great deal, Arthur. Moral standards, a code of behaviour, Christian beliefs. But I'm certainly not going to try and explain my philosophy to you now! Come along, Carol. We're going to get packed.

                (*He marches out of the saloon.* CAROL *pulls a wry face to the others.*)

CAROL   Come on, Wendy. We'd better do as he says.

WENDY   I'm more or less ready.

CAROL   Sorry, everyone.

                (CAROL *follows* JOHN *to their cabin.*)

ARTHUR   Oh dear. Well I'm sorry the trip has been a bit of a trial for you, Wendy.

WENDY   (*closing her suitcase*) Oh, but it's been the best weekend I've had for years, Mr Bullhead.

ARTHUR   Really? Oh, well that's something.

WENDY   I think I'll always remember it.

ARTHUR   Yes - well I hope it doesn't leave you with too much to remember it by.

MARY	(*sharply*) Arthur!
ARTHUR	Sorry.
SHIRLEY	(*to* WENDY) Want to come up on deck while you're waiting, Wend? Make the most of the sun.
WENDY	All right.
MARY	No going off again, mind, Shirley. They'll be wanting to leave soon.

(*The girls go up on deck. Next door,* JOHN *has opened the suitcases and is throwing things into them.* CAROL *helps, more calmly.*)

JOHN	(*suddenly bursting out*) I can't understand it! I just can't understand it, Carol.

(*In the saloon,* ARTHUR *and* MARY *hear the sound of his outburst, and look at each other.* ARTHUR *sneaks to the wall to listen.* MARY *follows more discreetly.*)

CAROL	What?
JOHN	How could you do it? You were positively condoning that dreadful family's attitudes. You've been practically a conspirator in all their appalling machinations.
CAROL	Machinations?
JOHN	Well, what else would you call them? This whole weekend has been one long subterfuge designed to undermine our entire way of life. They're the most amoral bunch of people I've ever come across.
CAROL	Oh, I wouldn't say that.
JOHN	Oh, you wouldn't, eh?
CAROL	No.

JOHN   And what would you call them? Eh?

CAROL   Just a fairly ordinary family trying to muddle through like the rest of us.

JOHN   (*appalled*) Like the rest . . . !

MARY   (*next door*) I don't think we should listen to this, Arthur.

ARTHUR   (*gesturing at her*) Shhhh. I can't hear.

            (MARY *sets her jaw, and leaves the saloon towards the cabins.*)

JOHN   Carol, they have threatened my livelihood; they've tried to blackmail me into what amounts to criminal procedures; they've destroyed the years of moral teaching we've instilled into Wendy, and compromised her chances of making a good marriage . . .

CAROL   Oh don't be ridiculous!

JOHN   Ridiculous? What do you mean, ridiculous? She's . . .

CAROL   Are you trying to tell me that, in this modern day and age, no one who isn't a virgin has a chance of making a good marriage? You've just disqualified ninety five per cent of the unmarried population.

JOHN   You may deride my so-called old-fashioned moral beliefs, Carol, but let me tell you the world was a lot better place when they were more widely practised. Look at the degeneracy of the young, look at AIDS, look at . . .

CAROL   Oh phooey! Was the Black Death, and cancer, and . . . and Pearl Harbour all due to moral degeneracy?

JOHN
Pearl Harbour? What on earth . . . ? Look, this conversation's getting off the point. I'm talking about us! The decent, caring example our family has always stood for . . .

CAROL
You mean the stuffy, pompous, holier-than-thou example. It's no wonder we haven't any real friends. It's no wonder nobody asks us to anything except church coffee mornings and fund-raising events for Save The Whale!

JOHN
Oh, I suppose you'd rather they invited us to local wife-swapping parties . . . ?

CAROL
Yes! Yes, I would!

JOHN
Carol!

CAROL
Anything to bring a bit of reality, and spontaneity, and . . . and . . . *fun* into our existence!

JOHN
Fun! Carol, what are you saying? After all these years of happy married life . . .

CAROL
Who says it was a happy married life? Eh? When have you ever asked me if I've been happy in our married life?

JOHN
Of course you have! I've always loved you. I've given you everything you've needed . . .

CAROL
Yes, but when have you ever given me anything I've *wanted*?

JOHN
Wanted?

CAROL
Yes - wanted, desired, hungered for? (*Strides up and down.*) I haven't realised it myself up to now, I've been so indoctrinated by your prissy moral posturing - but this weekend has really opened my eyes. I've seen life as Wendy must see it - as I used to see it when I was her age - with all the chances, and the excitement, and the romance ahead of her . . .

JOHN   But we're not Wendy's age any more, Carol.
            We're mature, responsible adults, with . . .

CAROL   Does that mean we've got to stop living?
            We've got to forget passion, and joy, and
            adventure . . . ?

JOHN   Passion for what? Adventure where?

CAROL   Adventure here and now - like having a boat,
            and sneaking off for naughty weekends on it . . .

JOHN   Naughty weekends!

CAROL   Passion for good food and wine and all the
            other nice things that are supposed to be bad
            for you. Joy in . . . in sex!

JOHN   Sex?

CAROL   Yes.

JOHN   We enjoy sex.

CAROL   No, we don't. We go through the dutiful
            motions of it, like cleaning our teeth, and
            washing the car on Sundays. I'm talking
            about real, glorious, gutsy, bonking!

JOHN   (*almost fainting*) Carol!

CAROL   Like I had with that painter on my parent's
            drawing room floor all those years ago. And
            like I suspect Wendy got from her
            thoroughbred stud last night.

JOHN   (*sitting weakly on the bed*) Oh my God!

CAROL   Look at you! Totally devastated by the idea
            that your own daughter might be a human
            being. What role in life had you in mind for
            her, eh? A latter day Virgin Mary?

JOHN   Of course not.

CAROL   Then some modern, tight-arsed feminist who
               hates all men? D'you know, John, I'm really
               seeing you . . . no, not you - us, for the first
               time. All these years I've gone along with
               the charade. I've thought, how lucky we are.
               What an example of all that family life should
               be. What a wonderful husband, standing for
               everything that is strong, and sensible, and
               right. And what a perfect wife I must be, to
               be able to live up to him. Yugh! When deep
               down all I really wanted was to be part of one
               of those corny TV commercials, where the
               almost naked girl strides dripping out of a
               tropical sea, to the strains of Mahler, to where
               a bronzed gorilla waits on the beach for her
               with a Bacardi in each hand, and a bathing
               costume about to split at the seams with lust!

               (*Long pause.*)

JOHN   (*eventually*) I can't think of anything to say.

CAROL   Good! Your silence is infinitely preferable to
               your pompous platitudes. I'll be on deck
               when you're ready to leave.

               (*Turns, and leaves the cabin.* ARTHUR
               *hurriedly leaves his listening post, and takes
               up a casual pose in the armchair.* CAROL
               *enters the saloon, and starts to cross to the
               outside door. Then she becomes aware of his
               studied air of disinterest, and stops.*)

CAROL   I suppose you heard all that?

ARTHUR   (*innocently*) What, Carol?

CAROL   Well, it doesn't matter. It's high time we
               came out into the open. Did I hear Mary
               mention coffee earlier?

ARTHUR   (*starting to rise*) Yes, I'll get you some.

CAROL   (*waving him back*) Stay there - I'm quite
               capable of pouring my own.

(*Goes to the galley area.*)

Well, I can't say I've really *enjoyed* this
weekend, Arthur - but I wouldn't have missed
it for anything. It's been an education.

ARTHUR   Oh, well that's something, I suppose.
(*Glances towards the door.*) Er . . . all of it?

CAROL   (*returning with a cup of coffee*) All?

ARTHUR   (*nodding at the roof above him*) Last night as
well?

CAROL   (*sitting*) Oh yes. That as well.

ARTHUR   Oh good. I'd hate to think . . . I don't want
you to get the wrong idea . . . things are
pretty good between me and Mary really. I
couldn't do without the old girl. And no one
else would live with me for long. But now
and again . . . well, it's good to have a bit of
romance, to remind you what it's all about.

CAROL   Yes. Exactly.

ARTHUR   I'm just sorry the girls came back when they
did.

CAROL   Oh, I think perhaps that was just as well. We
wouldn't have wanted things to have gone too
far, would we?

ARTHUR   Yes.

CAROL   (*laughing*) Arthur - you're impossible.

ARTHUR   Still - it's a good memory to have. I'd hate to
get old without a few good memories. The
feel of your . . . of your breast is a very good
memory.

CAROL   (*fighting off sudden tears*) Oh, Arthur . . .

ARTHUR   (*nervous*) Here, don't . . . (*Gives her his handkerchief.*)

CAROL   (*wiping her eyes*) It's all right. I'm just being silly.

              (MARY *reappears in the cabin, and* ARTHUR *hastily takes back his handkerchief.* MARY *casually takes in the situation, and goes to the galley area.*)

MARY   Is Arthur looking after you all right, Carol?

CAROL   Oh, yes thank you, Mary.

MARY   (*pouring herself some coffee*) Well, I'm sorry you're off so soon. It's a lovely afternoon. We could have gone rowing on the river, or something - couldn't we, Arthur?

ARTHUR   Well, we could. But I think we've been in enough deep water for one weekend, don't you, dear? Ha, ha.

CAROL   John always likes to be back in good time anyway. To get ready for the week ahead. Talking of which, I think perhaps I ought to tell you, Arthur . . .

ARTHUR   What?

CAROL   There's no need for any bribes - or blackmails - over your supermarket scheme. It's almost certain to go through anyway. John told me last night.

ARTHUR   Really?

CAROL   So you can keep 'The Bunty'. And I hope you'll keep his little secret as well. I couldn't forgive myself if it got out.

MARY   What secret's that?

ARTHUR   Oh, just a business secret between me and
                Carol, love. (*To* CAROL.) But what about
                John's threats to stop the scheme? I somehow
                don't think he'll be very keen to see it go
                through after . . . all that's happened.

CAROL   He will. I'll see to it.

                (*Next door*, JOHN *closes the suitcases, and
                leaves the cabin with them.*)

ARTHUR   Well, in that case - I should see to it that you
                have *some* sort of reward. Even if it's not as
                obvious as 'The Bunty'. Perhaps a nice
                discreet little motor cruiser . . . second-
                hand . . . that nobody would notice.

CAROL   That would be very nice.

                (*They grin at each other.* JOHN *enters the
                saloon with the suitcases. He takes in the
                scene.*)

JOHN   Carol - it's time we were leaving.

MARY   Oh, have a cup of coffee before you go, John.
                We're all having one.

JOHN   Well, I'd rather . . .

CAROL   (*emphatically*) I'm staying to finish my
                coffee, John - so you might as well.

JOHN   (*unhappily*) Oh. Well, all right.

                (MARY *gets him some coffee. He turns to*
                ARTHUR *with barely controlled anger.*)

                I think I should say, Arthur . . .

ARTHUR   In all honesty?

JOHN   (*gritting his teeth*) I think I should say that I
                will never forgive you for what you've done

to me and my family this weekend. You have
almost destroyed eighteen years of happy
married life in less than twenty four hours.

ARTHUR   Oh dear, John - that's dreadful. I didn't know
I had such power.

JOHN   Scarcely an angry word has passed between us
in all that time, and now suddenly we're
fighting over . . . over straightforward moral
issues that we've accepted without question
before.

CAROL   John . . .

JOHN   No, Carol - let me have my say. And it seems
to me, Arthur, that the reason is - and I have
to say it - the example set by you and your
family, which has led mine astray, and made
them question all that we have, up till now,
held dear.

ARTHUR   You don't think . . . ?

JOHN   What?

ARTHUR   Well, that perhaps a few things *needed*
questioning? I'm not criticising, mind. And
I'm certainly not defending my family as a
paragon of virtue. But don't you feel that
perhaps it's a bit *odd* that you've never had
the occasional argy-bargy in eighteen years?

JOHN   Why should we? If one is agreed on one's
principles in life, what is there to argue
about?

ARTHUR   Ah well - you're a lucky man indeed, John, if
you're that certain of your principles. I wish
I was.

JOHN   Yes, well . . . if I may say so, Arthur, you
might perhaps fare a little happier if you gave
some serious thought to such things. It's a

question of considering the general good before your own personal benefit. Something you learn as a town councillor.

ARTHUR   Hmm. I'll tell you something, John, that might surprise you. I was a councillor once.

JOHN   You?

ARTHUR   Yeh. Me. Hard to imagine, isn't it? But when I was twenty eight, all starry-eyed and full of the crusading spirit, I became the Tory councillor for the South West ward of our little town. I lasted two years.

JOHN   Got kicked out at the next election, eh?

ARTHUR   No. I resigned.

JOHN   Why?

ARTHUR   I couldn't stand working with such a bunch of wankers.

          (JOHN recoils.)

MARY   Arthur!

ARTHUR   Of which you - if I might say so - are a prime example.

JOHN   How dare you!

ARTHUR   You see, John, I soon reached the conclusion that very few of the people on the council - whether of the left or the right - were there in order to do a good job of work. Most of them, I realised, were either there because they reckoned the title of Councillor would put them one up on their neighbours . . . or because they wanted a platform on which to air their prejudices . . . or simply because they were bored with life and got a few kicks in the council chamber.

CAROL

Which category are you suggesting John falls in?

ARTHUR

Oh, a bit of all of them, I reckon. Anyway, I soon found that it's impossible to debate things rationally amongst that lot. There's such a din from the posturers and the pontificators and the bigots and the belly-achers, that anyone who's trying to get to the genuine heart of the matter never gets a look in. I soon realised that the real talent in the community lies with people who wouldn't be seen dead in the bloody council chamber! For one thing they don't have the time - they're too busy getting on with their own thing, usually having to fight the council all the way in the process. And for another they don't have the patience to deal with such a bunch of second-rate wallies in any case.

JOHN

Thank you. Making a mockery of public service is just what I'd expect from you.

MARY

Arthur, don't be so tactless.

ARTHUR

Not tactless, Mary, just frank. Shall I tell you who *finally* made me see the light, John? Any more coffee in that pot, love?

(MARY *moves to pour him some.* JOHN *is staring at him in speechless paralysis.*)

Eh, shall I?

MARY

Well you're going to anyway, so get on with it.

ARTHUR

(*with an irritable glance at her*) Our old friend, Jack Craddock. Yes. It was the time when the council had just refused his application for a petrol station on the West side of town - which was needed, he quite rightly said, because of increased traffic, and to stop people driving through the centre of town to fill up at one of the others. It was kicked out partly because the chairman of planning at that time *owned* most of the others, and partly because half the council didn't like Jack Craddock and all he stood for. Well, Jack said to me afterwards, 'Arthur', he said, 'don't waste time farting around with council work. You do best for the community by doing best for yourself.' And he went on to prove it. He caught them all with their pants down by putting up an ultra-modern petrol station in record time, just outside the town boundary - undercutting everyone else's prices, and doing such a roaring trade he'd pinched half the chairman's own business before the man knew what was happening. But of course you know about that. You had something to do with that project, if I remember.

(JOHN *fidgets uncomfortably*.)

MARY   Did you, John? I didn't know you had anything to do with petrol stations.

JOHN   (*testily*) You consider that simply winning a cut throat petrol pump war is proof of moral rectitude, do you?

ARTHUR   No. I consider it's a proof of expediency. Which in most cases is the best we can hope for.

JOHN   That's a pretty unambitious aim.

ARTHUR   Oh, I agree. But then, on the whole, it's a pretty unambitious world. Once in a while someone comes along with the genius to push something through that makes a *real* difference to things - but very rarely. And invariably in the teeth of opposition from their local council.

MARY   Can we change the subject now, Arthur?

ARTHUR	Shall I tell you, John . . . ?
MARY	Silly question.
ARTHUR	Shall I tell you what I think ought to happen over the schools and the supermarket scheme?
JOHN	We all know what *you* think ought to happen.
ARTHUR	No, you don't. What I *really* think ought to happen is that both the schools are left where they are, even if you have to reduce their numbers a bit.
JOHN	I thought you didn't think much of Collier's school.
ARTHUR	Oh I grumble, but it's not bad as schools go. No, they're both pretty good as a matter of fact - and the reason is they keep each other on their toes. The moment you take one away there'll be no competition, and you can bet your shirt the other one'll go straight to the dogs.
JOHN	Well if you kept the schools, there wouldn't be a site for the supermarket.
ARTHUR	Yes, there would. There's the Old Market site.
JOHN	That's impracticable. Too many problems. You said so yourself.
ARTHUR	It is for Garrett's. They haven't the imagination to see how to go about it. But Craddock has.
JOHN	Craddock? I thought he was your rival. I thought you didn't like him.
ARTHUR	I don't. He's a right bastard. But he builds great supermarkets.
JOHN	Concrete monstrosities, you called them.

ARTHUR   That's just telling you what you wanted to
         hear. Actually he puts up bloody marvellous
         shops, does Craddock. I bet you he'd take
         that wasted hunk of land and build a temple
         there that would be seen for miles around.
         It'd be a magnet for every housewife in the
         county.

MARY   (*nodding to* CAROL) Mmm.

ARTHUR   You see - the girls would go. But the council
         would never buy a vision like that. Getting
         that one past you lot would be like pissing
         into the wind. Which seems to leave the field
         free to me really - doesn't it? (*Pause.*) More
         coffee, John?

JOHN   (*white with anger*) I'll be buggered if I'll let
         you get your scheme through, Bullhead!

CAROL   John!

ARTHUR   Language, John!

JOHN   Do what you like with your miserable bit of
         information on me. I'll fight you tooth and
         nail through every stage, until you'll wish
         you'd never heard of Garrett's and their
         blasted supermarkets. I'll make you piss into
         so much wind you'll drown in it!

MARY   (*mildly*) Oh dear, John - that doesn't sound
         like you.

JOHN   No, Mary - it doesn't sound like me. Thanks
         to your husband I hardly know who me is any
         more. My entire world has been turned on its
         head by that evil man.

MARY   Oh come now, John - I won't have you calling
         my husband evil. He may be a pain in the
         arse, but he's not evil.

JOHN	I'll reserve judgement on that. (*Picks up the suitcases.*) Where's Wendy, Carol?
CAROL	Up on deck, I think, but . . .
JOHN	Bring her suitcase. We're leaving.
CAROL	Hold on, John, I think we . . .
JOHN	(*apoplectic*) Do as you're told, woman! I will not have any more argument! Bring that case, and don't say another word until we're off this bloody boat!

(*He storms out of the saloon and up to the fore-deck, where the girls have been alerted by the shouting.*)

CAROL	Astonishing! He hasn't shown such passion in years. (*Picks up the case.*)
JOHN	Wendy - we're leaving. Follow me.
WENDY	But . . .
JOHN	(*roaring*) *Now!*

(*Storms off the boat and along the bank.*)

| CAROL | Thank you both for a . . . a memorable weekend. |

(*They smile and wave, and she goes up on deck.*)

WENDY	'Bye, Shirley. See you back at school.
SHIRLEY	Yeah.
WENDY	(*smiling*) It's been a great weekend - for me anyway.
SHIRLEY	(*smiling back*) Me too.

CAROL   Goodbye, Shirley.

SHIRLEY   'Bye.

                 (CAROL and WENDY follow JOHN off along the
                 river bank. SHIRLEY goes below to the cabin.)

ARTHUR   They gone?

SHIRLEY   Yeah. What did you say to him, Dad? He
                 looked as if he had a rocket up his bum.

ARTHUR   Oh, just told him a few home truths. Well,
                 Mary love - looks as if we'll have to say
                 goodbye to our dreams of a nice easy
                 retirement.

MARY   Could he stop your scheme going through?

ARTHUR   I wouldn't be surprised. That sort can fight
                 very dirty when they're pushed.

MARY   Oh well . . . we're not so badly off, are we?

ARTHUR   No. And we can always sell 'The Bunty' of
                 course. Not the same, but it'd fetch quite a
                 bit.

MARY   I thought you said it was worth nearly nothing
                 on the books.

ARTHUR   Oh, there are ways round that.

MARY   Arthur . . . He's right, you know - you *are*
                 wicked.

ARTHUR   (*grinning, and putting his arm round her*) I'm
                 no saint - but at least I'm not a bloody
                 hypocrite, eh? Well, now - what are we going
                 to do with ourselves? The weekend isn't over
                 yet. Got anything nice for supper, have we,
                 love?

MARY   We've got those frozen canellonis you said
                were rubbish and a waste of money.

ARTHUR   Oh, lovely. I like Italian. (*To* SHIRLEY.) That
                lad of yours around, Shirley - Darren, is it?

SHIRLEY   I could probably find him.

ARTHUR   Yes - ask him round for dinner. I'd like to
                have a chat with him about boats and so forth.

SHIRLEY   (*happily*) Right.

ARTHUR   Mind you, if you get up to any funny business
                with him on the bank afterwards . . . don't
                frighten the ducks.

SHIRLEY   (*grinning*) No, Dad.

ARTHUR   (*putting his feet up, and stretching
                luxuriously*) Oh, this is nice. Sunday
                afternoon on the river - all by ourselves.
                Peace and privacy - lovely!

MARY   Yes.

                (*Pause.*)

ARTHUR   Funny family, that, eh?

MARY   Yes.

ARTHUR   Most peculiar. Still, it takes all sorts . . .

                (*Shakes his head to himself, and drinks his
                coffee.*)

                Blackout.